If I'm God's Handiwork, Would Someone Please Explain These Thighs!

Discovering Your Unique Destiny

Cathy Lechner

OLIVER
NELSON
™

THOMAS NELSON PUBLISHERS®
Nashville

A Division of Thomas Nelson, Inc.
www.ThomasNelson.com

Published in Nashville, Tennessee, by Thomas Nelson, Inc.

Library of Congress Cataloging-in-Publication Data

Lechner, Cathy.
    If I'm God's handiwork, would someone please explain these thighs : discovering
your unique destiny / Cathy Lechner.
      p. cm.
   ISBN 0-7852-6838-3 (pbk.)
    1. Christian women—Religious life. 2. Lechner, Cathy. I. Title.
BV4527 .L435 2003
248.8'43—dc21   2002000730

Printed in the United States of America

02 03 04 05 06 PHX 5 4 3 2 1

I lovingly dedicate this book to my papa and mama in the ministry

Bishop Bill
and
Evelyn "Mom" Hamon

Thank you for taking the time to teach us, for bearing the price of being a prophetic voice in the church to this generation—never judging but always embracing those of us who hungered for a "word." You never despised us; you understood that our hearts were right. Your sacrifice did not go unnoticed by God or by us, your spiritual children. May this book be an honor to your kindness and a testament to your faithfulness.

Contents

Introduction

Beloved, here we are at the beginning of a great journey, you and I and the Lord (as well as six of my children screaming in the background). We are about to have an exciting adventure.

I write from my heart, so I always ask the Lord, "What would I like to read as a wife, mother, minister, director of finance, carpool president, or the chief stockholder of Toys"R"Us?" The list goes on and on. On this occasion my simple prayer was answered simply— I felt an urgency in my spirit to write to you dear women about our need to run with the dream that God places in our hearts.

I am saddened by the thought that so many women have no dreams. They think that *unique* is a word that can be applied to a couple of other women they know, but for them, *ordinary* is the operative word. No matter that the Scriptures teach that we are called and chosen by God, uniquely selected to be His by birth and then by His gracious redemption in Christ.

Notice the title of this book, *If I'm God's Handiwork, Would Someone Please Explain These Thighs!* The fact is, we all have our imperfections—thighs, hips, and pouting lips—but they don't disqualify us. Ladies, we all have a destiny to fulfill, a dream to capture and actively participate in for His praise and our enjoyment. That's the reason for the subtitle, *Discovering Your Unique Destiny.* I hope you will journey with me through the pages of this little book so I can encourage you to move up to a new level of faith and confidence in His special, unique plan for you.

May the Holy Spirit encourage you and cause you to laugh at life (and yourself) again. As you enjoy some of my foibles and unbelievable adventures, perhaps you will breathe a sigh of relief when you realize you are not alone on your destiny journey. I hope you have as good a time reading this as I have had writing it.

Of course, it's not Watchman Nee, which I had to read in college. But I didn't have to spend twenty-five years in a Chinese prison either (which you and I know we couldn't possibly do without a phone and a place to plug in the curling iron; after all, there is only so much suffering a tortured author can do).

Let the adventure begin.

Love,
Cathy

Chapter One

The Brighter the Light, the More Bugs You Attract

Thank God for the many women who realize that they have a unique role to play in the kingdom of God. They see their calling, and they intentionally live to fulfill it. Inevitably those women learn that the journey they undertake is never an easy one. There are always so many obstacles to hinder them from achieving their objectives, yet with God's help, they can learn to be victorious. In this chapter I want to talk about some of these obstacles, some of the crazy, painful, and oftentimes funny situations that threaten our success and challenge our commitments to our King.

A Prolonged "Moment"

It was one of those rare moments . . . okay, I'm lying. It was actually a "moment" that I had been going through about four months.

I found myself thousands of miles away from home on foreign soil, the speaker at a very large conference, and I was having to deal with sorrowful news. A trusted member of our ministry staff, a man who had been like a son to us, was leaving.

Everyone leaves at some point, but he was leaving angry and frustrated, having said incredibly unkind words. My spirit wilted as I mentally rehashed the conversation, hearing the bitter words in my mind again and again. Exercising my soul to forgive, and then forgive again and again, I lay hopeless on the lumpy motel bed.

There is no hurt quite like the hurt and disappointment of a fellow Christian with a hammer and some nails in his hands (followed by a man with a cross who says, "Where do you want this?").

King David, the sweet psalmist of Israel, said it best: "Those who betray me are the same ones who went into the house of God to worship with me" (Ps. 55:13–14, author's paraphrase).

My husband deals with these things much better than I do. For thirty minutes I emoted over the cell phone. At four dollars a minute, my hurt was becoming overwhelmingly expensive.

"Honey, just throw it off. Don't take it personally," he said.

But I do, and I know that I'm not alone. It's hard to separate your heart from your head. That is precisely why Jesus commanded us to forgive "from your heart" (Matt. 18:35 NIV).

During the day I was occupied by ministry, lunch meetings, service preparations, book signings, and press interviews, which kept my mind busy. But late at night, in the dark quiet of the motel room, those angry, judging accusations invaded my sleep.

There I lay, pitifully angry, having an imaginary conversation with my accuser (which is really weird when you are seven thousand miles from home). I had a perfect answer for every accusation and lie, justifying myself with great indignation to horrible red-and-yellow faded drapery. (I always seem to think of a really snappy comeback long after the offending party has moved on.)

Salty tears began to roll down my cheeks. I didn't try to stop them. Their taste in my mouth reflected the same bitterness that was in my gut.

"Help me! Help me, God!" I cried. Four months of deep hurt and all the oppression that comes with it seemed to spill out onto the dirty green carpet.

Usually I would not have dared to get down on the floor of the hotel room. I can barely stand my own carpets when they are filthy. But this was now holy ground, and the five-by-six space became His throne room.

Then God spoke.

Now please don't close the book. I promise you that I'm not a "granola" Christian— fruity, flaky, and nutty. God still speaks today. He spoke to me. It wasn't audible, but I heard Him nonetheless. This is what He said: *Daughter, warfare is simply a sign that you are making progress.*

The tears stopped, and my head snapped up in bewilderment. Grabbing the pen from the nightstand, I began to write.

You have literally bombarded the gates of hell with the power and the might that are inside you, and the enemy has risen up and said, *"You are not going to make it because I will make you fail and fall." So, my precious daughter, expect something* great!

It is so hard to lay down your life when you are attacked! Especially difficult are the moments when the challenge comes from a close friend and confidant or a fellow worker in the ministry. These occasions, however, offer wonderful opportunities to learn to rely fully on the God who wants to comfort and strengthen you on the journey.

"I Just Adored Your Message"

For those of us who have a ministry of teaching the Word, another frequent problem occurs when some of the audience seem to be permanent conference attendees. They go to every meeting that comes to town or the surrounding region, but they never actually receive the Word in such a way that significant change and permanent transformation take place in their lives.

If you are anything like me, you go to a conference or revival meeting and get saturated with the Word. You leave feeling you will never be the same, and you make a lot of promises that you fully intend to keep.

But not everyone receives the Word in that way. Some are too busy measuring one speaker against another. Rather than embracing the message that the speaker tries to bring, these people compare the sermon to others they have heard. I have preached my heart out, only to hear, "What a great word, Cathy, but you should have heard Gloria Copeland preach it. I can get you a tape. You might really learn something from it." My face is frozen in an idiotic smile, and I wonder as I stand there whether God would forgive me just this once if my hand "accidentally" smacked her.

Of course, one of my favorite backhanded compliments is, "Loved your message, Mrs. Lechner."

"Oh, really? What did you love most about it?"

The person then registers that deer-in-the-headlights look, and I can see her involuntarily swallow. "Well, let's see . . . I think it was . . . um . . . the part . . . the Bible and God . . . um . . ."

Yes, that person really adored my message! There are two dangers here. One is for the speaker, who could become cynical and subtly allow unbelief and internal questions about the adequacy of God's message to invade her heart and mind as she sees people responding glibly to God's message. The other danger is for those who attend these conferences and fail to come to terms with the claims of God on their lives.

Breakthrough Means You Must . . . Break Through!

Everyone knows that when you buy a new car, a new home, or even a new office, you receive a new key. You add the key to your key ring so you will have access to it when needed.

I have old keys on my key chain and absolutely no recollection of what they belong to. I'm afraid to throw them away because the minute I do, I'll learn one of them is the key that opens an old dead relative's treasure chest worth half a million dollars. I still have my skate key from my birthday skates when I was eight. I also have the key to my diary, where I professed my love of an older man, Rudy Forester, a fifth grader. Of course, I have no idea where the diary is.

One day, on my way to a lunch appointment, I was late—as usual. With the same intensity that I have prayed for people with life-threatening cancer, I prayed diligently for a close parking spot. Maybe that is why I had to finally settle for a space practically in the next state. Grabbing my purse and opening the door, I hit the lock button and slammed it shut in one hasty move.

No sooner had the door closed and locked, to my utter dismay, I remembered the keys. There they were, in the ignition, mocking me.

There would be no two-hour leisurely lunch that day. Instead, I spent the two hours waiting for AAA to open my car door. People passed by every five minutes asking if I needed help. Embarrassed, I told them my sad story. I'm sure they laughed their heads off as soon as they could safely mock me.

Oh, how we love to get a "word" from God. Our miracle of finances comes in or a backslidden husband comes to the Lord, and we are encouraged.

But immediately the enemy comes to steal it away. We slam the door and forget the "key." It was the key for our breakthrough.

If you desire a lasting change, if you desperately need a break-through, then you must put a demand on the anointing that God has put within you. You must pick up the key that you received during that conference, that revival, or that time you spent at Jesus' feet in prayer, and begin to use it. You are responsible for holding on to that breakthrough, for unlocking the door to victory in your life. If you do not make the effort, you will remain the same.

The Devil Is Not a Wall; He Is a Door

Another tool God uses to challenge and perfect us is the presence of difficult people in our lives. I am not predisposed to trials and tribulations. My idea of suffering is having my hair pulled through a frosting cap. But a smooth sea never makes a skilled mariner. Unless we are living with challenge, unless we are willing to be stretched, we will stagnate. We were born with eternity on our hearts. We were born to think BIG! If we refuse a challenge, we spoil.

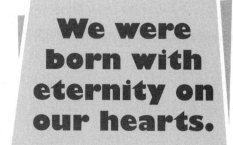

We were born with eternity on our hearts.

God chooses enemies to challenge us. He uses enemies to change us. God wants us to go beyond what we thought we could do in our everyday living.

If Your Dreams Don't Frighten You, You're Dreaming Too Small

Eight and a half months pregnant, I was trying so hard to be the dutiful pastor's wife. I was leading worship, teaching children's church, and preparing Communion. The last thing I wanted on Monday morning was a phone call from the crabbiest member of our congregation. An elderly Jewish woman who had been interned at Auschwitz, she came to our messianic synagogue for the free food we had on Friday nights.

"I'm sick. Come over now and help me," she demanded.

Sweetly I answered, "Greta, I'm throwing up; my back hurts; my legs are swollen. I just can't. I'll send someone else."

"No! I want you. And bring some soup from the kosher deli." *Click.*

You old bat! I thought as I hauled my beached-whale body out of my warm bed, went to the store to buy all the fixings for home-made matzo ball soup, and headed for Greta's condo. Images of my husband snoring in our bed added to my foul mood.

Bless God, I am going to love that crotchety old woman into the kingdom if I have to give birth on her kitchen table.

I used my nesting instinct to clean the entire condominium, top to bottom. I put the soup on to cook and then hauled her pile of dirty clothes downstairs to the laundry room. And, yes, I used my own quarters.

While giving her a sponge bath, combing her hair, and fluffing her pillows, I felt an awesome sense of pride and accomplishment. Carefully I raised the spoon to her mouth, feeling extremely right-eous after five hours of household labor.

Then it happened. Greta made an awful face, spit out the soup, and cried, "It's too salty!"

The heat rose up in my cheeks and I started to cry. Hormones, lots of them, were doing laps through my body.

Suddenly the Spirit of God rose up within me with such mercy and compassion that I was surprised. I saw her as the Lord saw her, a frightened little girl who once had to fight just to stay alive, a young widow who lost all her family in the Holocaust. My tears for my own sorry self became tears of love and mercy for this poor lost soul. We embraced, and I held her like a child until her tears came.

We led her to her Messiah, Yeshua-Jesus, months later, just weeks before she went home to be with the Lord.

It was a lesson I never forgot. If you are not willing to be stretched and move from where you are in God, even to the place of adjusting your lifestyle if need be out of your sheer love for

Jesus, then in all probability you have already absorbed all the truth you can handle.

God uses difficult people in our lives to keep us on our knees. Marriage is the most perfect tool created to knock everything off us that does not look like Jesus. God uses children to drive out the selfishness that binds up our stubborn hearts. It's hard to ignore the screams of an infant every hour on the hour.

We can hear "Love your enemies and do good to them that persecute you" until, like a sponge, we're saturated with it. But the only thing that makes the sponge usable is wringing it out. Every bit of moisture must be forced out violently to make it of any use again.

When we hear and hear and hear truth and we don't act on it, then we can't receive anymore. We memorize the Word, but there is nowhere to store it in our hearts unless we are continually sharing His life and love, through our time, talents, and resources, with someone else.

Don't limit God to your natural abilities and natural resources.

I can think of nothing sadder than getting to heaven and having only a rhinestone Jesus pin to toss at His feet. I imagine Jesus pulling out a blueprint of my life and comparing it to what I actually did in His name, then seeing how far I missed the mark of His original plan—all because I didn't exercise the faith or lacked the dedication to humble myself and obey.

You Can Stand Pressure If You Have Purpose

A man who took up golfing went out and bought the best equipment money could buy. He teed off, and the first ball landed in an ant bed. Dashing to the ant bed, he swung his club and killed five thousand ants. Swinging again, he killed four thousand more. One of the surviving ants looked at another and said, "If we're going to live, we'd better get on the ball."

Randi and I live under a continual challenge. We get through one thing and then find we're reaching for another. But if we're going to survive the challenges, we have to "get on the ball."

It's not just a talking faith or a walking faith. It's a running faith! And I find that 90 percent of all battles are won by just getting up and pressing on when I feel like going to bed with a Pepsi and eating Godiva chocolates.

Chapter Two

If I'm So Good, Where Is Everybody?

Scars are part of the battle. It's true, but often our scars are self-inflicted. We create the scenario that leads to our getting into trouble and the eventual scarring that may stay with us for a lifetime.

Sixteen years ago, I was a pastor's wife in a small town. My husband, Randi, and I had an eight-year-old daughter, but we desperately wanted more children.

A woman in our church was working with an unmarried young woman who had just found out she was pregnant. Her options were to abort the baby or find a good home for the child.

Desperate, I made all the necessary phone calls and arranged to meet the young woman at the attorney's office to finalize the adoption papers. All the time I had been making the calls and preparing the papers, a gnawing feeling kept me from the joy I so intensely wanted in anticipation of a long-awaited promise.

The peace of God was just not there. In fact, I was troubled. Nevertheless, I wanted what I wanted, and I pushed away the nagging doubt.

On my way to sign the final papers, a pedestrian, not watching where he was going, stepped in front of my car, causing me to swerve to avoid hitting him.

It's amazing what goes through your mind in those few seconds before a tragic accident. I began to skid when I slammed on my brakes. *Do I turn into the skid, or do I turn the wheel in the opposite direction of the skid?* I thought, and that was pretty much the last thought I had before crossing the median, rolling down the embankment, and slamming into a telephone pole.

What is so funny is that the principle on which I based my decision about which way to turn the wheel is for *icy* roads. I live in Florida, and it was ninety-eight degrees that day.

Instinctively I threw up my arm to protect my face. The force of the impact threw me through the window on the passenger's side. The seat belt I wore jerked me back in with incredible force.

The next thing I remember is the most horrible pain as EMTs used the Jaws of Life to get me out of the car. They also had to cut off my clothes because they had become entangled in the twisted steel.

Diagnosed with a broken leg, fractured ribs and collarbone, and internal bleeding, I was being prepped for surgery when my husband arrived at the ER. By the way, I saw no one, not one doctor, who looked like George Clooney (George Jetson maybe, but definitely not George Clooney).

My sweetheart burst into the emergency room, took one look at me, and cried, "Oh, my poor baby! Look what the devil did to you!"

I told him, "That's right, honey. It was the devil, and it had absolutely nothing to do with my bad driving." (Please keep in mind that I was on drugs during this conversation.)

As they wheeled me out to surgery, my husband threw up his hand and said, "Wait, I'm going to pray for my wife." There were mild protests from the orderly and nurses in attendance, but you see, my husband is a big and fearless man.

He prayed a simple, powerful, faith-filled prayer: "Lord, we honor You. You are the God who has promised to heal us. Heal my precious wife. Thank You. Amen."

Even the orderly was choking back his tears. I never made it to surgery. A new set of X rays ordered by the neurologist showed no internal injuries and no broken bones. Of course, they wouldn't call it a miracle, just an aberration of the X rays. Okay . . . but I did have the glass picked out piece by piece from my arm with the use of the latest medical extraction equipment—tweezers. Sixty-four stitches and three days later, I was sent home.

There Would Have Been No Sneaking Home for Me

The officer who had been on the scene of the accident came to my house shortly afterward to return some things found in the car and to have me sign papers.

"I am so embarrassed," was my stupid comment to him.

Officer Stiffly looked at me and said, "Ma'am?"

"If it had not been for that dumb telephone pole, my car would have come to rest gently on the little canal. I could have gotten out and called the tow truck and sneaked home."

"Mrs. Lechner, I thought you knew," Officer Stiffly replied with furrowed brow, a law enforcement sign of very serious news. "The trajectory of your tire marks on the road [nice way of saying 'when you lost control and skidded all over the place'] indicated that you were up on two wheels as you went into the canal. The vehicle was starting to flip upside down, and you would have come to a rest submerged. Your neck would most likely have broken, and you would have drowned before anyone could have gotten to you." He looked down at his feet and continued, "The pole that you slammed into saved your life. Instead of turning upside down, the impact righted you."

I couldn't answer. I couldn't even breathe. The phone pole that I had been cursing and blaming for all my trouble and all my pain actually saved me.

And what about the baby I was so intent upon adopting as I careened off the road that day? The young woman whose baby I had so desperately wanted gave birth twelve weeks early. We didn't know she had been a heavy drinker and drug user during her pregnancy. The severely deformed, premature infant boy lingered a torturous long month before he finally died.

My heart is for children, and Randi and I have adopted six wonderful little ones since that sad time. But when I was arranging to adopt that little child, I had not been seeking God's guidance for the right timing for adding a child to our family. As sad as that story is, my disobedience almost ruined God's perfect will and plan for our lives. Had I made it to the attorney's office that afternoon, papers would have been signed that would have made us legally responsible for that woman's medical bills and the baby's as well. They amounted to hundreds of thousands of dollars, and we had no medical insurance to cover the costs.

The moral of the story is *not* that God throws His servants into telephone poles and almost kills us when we disobey. But when we turn a deaf ear to His voice of wisdom and reason in order to have what we want—when we want it—a piece of His divine wall of protection is lifted so that we can really see what it would be like if He allowed us to have what we *think* we can't live without.

That Internal Thermometer Is There for a Reason

God has given to all of us a "peace." Some call it conscience. But as spiritual people, we are admonished to let the "peace of God" keep our hearts and minds (Phil. 4:7). Colossians 3:15 tells us, "Let the peace of Christ rule in your hearts." He has given us an internal thermometer to gauge situations we may find ourselves in.

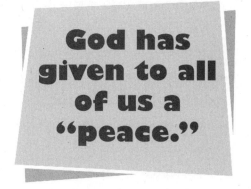

God has given to all of us a "peace."

My peace, my internal thermometer, was saying a huge "NO." But I went against the peace of God that was inside me, and it could have cost me my life. God, in His great mercy, kept me from making a very serious lifelong mistake. I thought the phone pole in my life was God's judgment, but it was actually His mercy.

The Father has an incredible destiny for us. Often our stubborn wills, not the devil, cause us to ruin our destinies. We do it to ourselves. Even mature, Jesus-living, sold-out Christians have blind spots where little pockets of disobedience rise up.

There were more babies, a lot more babies. I was just eight years too early because God's destiny includes His perfect timing. God's unique plan for us, however, does not necessarily include our "dream for the future." Listen to the story of this young woman.

Don't Expect a Fairy Tale

She was a gorgeous twenty-four-year-old woman who had been through a terrible marriage. She had a six-year-old child who, quite frankly, looked like Damien—the demon seed. If anyone tried to correct him, his eyes would roll to the top of his head, and he would begin to growl. I almost expected at any moment for his head to start spinning and for him to begin vomiting green bile. The young woman was lonely and needed help with her son, but she wouldn't date any of the "average" men who asked her out. She believed that some perfect man would show up and magically solve all her problems, financial and personal. I'll describe him to you.

He's six feet four inches tall and weighs about 195 pounds. He has coal-black hair and deep Mediterranean-blue eyes. His body was sculpted by Michelangelo, and he sports a year-round tan. No one can understand why because he is always hidden away in prayer. He speaks with a slight French-Israeli accent, and when he quotes the Word, which is often, fire comes out of his eyes.

Women faint around him (not under the power of the Holy Spirit), but he does not notice because he is way too spiritually minded. He is independently wealthy and spends his spare time at the piano in his library writing songs for his new CD, then pilots his private jet to developing countries to do brain surgery on the poor peasants.

Dr. Sloan Kincaid, a man of God, prophet, gifted neurosurgeon, Kenneth Copeland type—and that was who this whining girl couldn't live without.

There's only one thing wrong with that. Such a man doesn't exist. Your guy is about five feet eight-and-a-half inches tall in his loafers, and he wears those pants with a thirty-one-inch waist that fit under his belly. All is okay until he turns around and bends over. It's then that you remind yourself, *Oh, well, he's good with the kids, and that burgundy usher sports coat will cover all that up.*

His name, of course, is not Sloan, Stone, or Roan—it's Sid Bob. He's Billy Bob's twin brother.

Our wonderful destiny in God is not a fairy tale. Even when it begins to appear as one, we find that Dr. Sloan Kincaid is inordinately close to his mother, picks his nose in front of strangers, and still sleeps with his blankey.

Be thankful—at least your Sid Bob doesn't wear his leisure suits anymore.

See You at the Pole

Whether it is our haste to have or to do something that is not in God's plan or our search for a fairy-tale ending, sometimes it takes a phone-pole experience to get us going the right direction again. What is your telephone pole? What is your perceived enemy, the interruption in your life that seems to be delaying what you know should be the will of God? Will you still rejoice in spite of, and even because of, those enemies?

Scars are to remind you where you came from. I have sixty-four stitches in my right arm to remind me how very close I came to missing out on God's idea for perfect timing in growing my family. Seeing those scars comforts me with the knowledge of God's great mercy. He could squish me like an ant when I continue to disobey and complain because I don't understand why He won't give me what I want when I want it. Wah! Wah! Wah!

Instead He looks at this forty-six-year-old baby with love, mercy, and compassion, and we start all over. In the next chapter, you will begin to see what an incredible blessing enemies are in our lives. (Stop . . . come back! Keep on reading . . . PLEEEEASE??)

Sometimes it takes a phone-pole experience to get us going the right direction again.

Chapter Three

There's Victory in Jesus but Comfort in Cheesecake

W oman of God, it does not really matter where you have come from or what you are going through. The fact remains: *the past does not determine your future.* And you, child of God, have a future, an awesome future. But expect opposition.

Lord, Use My Enemy

I've said it a thousand times: "God, if I'm trying to do *Your* will— not mine, but *Yours*—and if I'm trying to bring souls into Your kingdom and be a blessing to others, then why does it seem as though there is so much opposition?"

Let me share with you a not-so-secret secret, a secret that took me so long to finally incorporate into my thinking that even my angel got discouraged: you will face opposition while pursuing your God-centered dreams, goals, and destiny. It's called *spiritual warfare*. Any attempt to thwart the eternal purposes of God involves spiritual warfare. Circumstances caused by human or supernatural opposition can create havoc and chaos in the lives of God's women who are fighting the good fight of faith. So, woman of God, be prepared to be opposed in fulfilling your destiny.

This is where your enemies come in.

Get a mental picture of the enemy standing in front of you. You know, the thing that is so insurmountable you can't possibly get through it alone. Write it down; enter it in your journal; jot it in the margins of this book. Read and reread this chapter as many times as you have to, and you will find that enemy will be destroyed. God is going to give you the tools and principles to conquer that troubling problem once and for all. You will walk out of your door in victory!

But it doesn't work like my favorite diet and exercise program. Years ago, my dear husband saw an ad for a miracle diet grapefruit pill on television. The ad ran from 4:00 to 4:30 A.M., basically when most normal people are supposed to be asleep. (I do allow for insomniacs, werewolves, and . . . my dear husband.)

What a diet! Take three grapefruit pills one half-hour before each meal and five at bedtime. Then go to sleep. That's it! When you wake up, BINGO! Your weight is gone. No dieting. No exercising. All the power is in the magic pill. The skinny fairy is supposed to smack you on the head with her magic size-six wand, but—surprise!—you're exactly the same. Well, not exactly. I had severe indigestion followed by constipation and then by horrible gas.

The secret of the diet is that if you smell bad enough, people will stand so far away from you that you'll appear much thinner.

I think we still have half a bottle of the grapefruit pills left. I'll let you have them for $19.95 plus $20.00 shipping and handling. It would be even better if you came and picked them up.

Why do I have so many left after all these years? Because they don't work.

We buy dozens of books and tapes, positive that they are going to magically change our lives and make us better with little or no effort. They are lies, I tell you, lies! All lies! . . . I guess that's a little dramatic.

The truth is, despite all of these self-help materials and quick fixes, your enemy will still oppose you. Just remember this: Satan's harassment is living proof that even he believes in your future. He knows you have something powerful inside you. Also remember that your enemy, be it spirit or human, is not a wall, but a door. The Lord has given you the key to open the door and walk through to victory.

I love James 1:2–3: "My brethren, count it all joy when you fall into various trials, knowing that the testing of your faith produces patience."

Misery is an option, but change is inevitable. So you determine how you go through change. Either you can be mad, miserable, and moody, or you can be trusting and joyous. But know this: if you wait long enough, your situation *will* change. Things will turn around for the better or for the worse. Also know that the spirit you choose to carry will affect those around you.

Others will be affected by the words you have spoken. The Bible warns that you should be careful what you say in your bedroom because "a bird of the air may carry your words, and a bird on the wing may report what you say" (Eccl. 10: 20 NIV).

We must all come to the same place. If God has not removed

that person or that situation from my life, no matter how much I have cried out to Him, then He wants me to exercise patience to build godly character. God is watching me to see if He can promote me. He wants to hear me (and you) say,

"Use my enemy to help me."
"Use my enemy to benefit me."

That's when God shows up. I can just imagine the Father watching from heaven and declaring to the angels and the twenty-four elders:

> **God is watching me to see if He can promote me.**

Look how My daughter loves Me. You know it's not easy. I saw her when she was weeping last night. But she rose up this morning, she lifted her hands to Me, and with tears flowing she declared in My hearing:

"God, I trust You. I love You. I will bless my enemy. I choose to forgive and do good to him."

Now go, angels, and bless My servant. She pleases me.

Of course, you have guessed that I have a vivid imagination!

Your enemies will defeat you, or you will get a breakthrough in spite of (and even because of) them.

It's a Benefit to Have an Enemy

Consider that your enemies are really there for your good. Now, that's positive thinking, and *you* have to speak it because no one else will do it for you. You are going to have to throw your own party. (One translation of James 1:2 declares that when you fall into heartbreaking trials, throw a party!)

One of the highest forms of faith is to laugh when you want to cry, to reach out and embrace others, to bring them into your home, your life, your party, when what you really want to do is to lie down on the couch and eat malted milk balls by the pound. Consider it all joy. Consider the end result of trials and tribulation as bringing great gladness to your life. Ask yourself as you walk through what seems like hell, *What is God looking for during these times? If He doesn't want to kill me but has a plan for my success, what am I missing?* Often, dear child of God, it is patience!

"Let patience have its perfect work, that you may be perfect and complete, lacking nothing" (James 1:4).

Character development and the enemies that bring me down are actually stepping-stones to climbing higher.

Learning patience has absolutely nothing to do with how many books of the Bible I have memorized. It has everything to do with responding to my enemies and those perceived situations. Character development and the enemies that bring me down are actually stepping-stones to climbing higher.

So the more enemies you have, the higher you go? Not necessarily. But the higher you go, the more enemies you'll certainly have.

Remember, *new levels bring new devils*.

I know a lot of Christians who get mad at people, mad at the church, mad at God, and then they get bitter. But God knows that adversaries have a way of stretching us. That is why God doesn't smite them, remove them, or kill us and take us to heaven. You are commanded to love your enemies. They may annoy you, even drive you crazy. But God will use them to develop your character.

So remember, you and I need enemies. They cause us to see how much of the love of Jesus we don't have. So zip your lip, fake it until you make it . . . but *love your enemies!*

See Through His Eyes

When you face opposition, when an enemy is in the camp, the wise woman seeks to understand the situation through God's perspective. It can be a critical mistake not to see your situation through God's eyes. Here's an example.

My husband and I were married only six weeks after we met. I don't recommend that unless you really believe it's God. We realized on our honeymoon that we knew practically nothing about each other.

The Honeymoon

We were up in the mountains of Franklin, North Carolina. I would rather have been on the beach or anywhere else. We were in a one-bedroom rustic cabin. *Rustic* is the kindest word I can find for *shack*. If we had had any money, I would have been at the Marriott. That's my idea of camping.

My beloved husband of one week announced that he would be preparing dinner that night. I panicked when I saw him take *all* of our honeymoon cash to the grocery store. I made a pretense of wanting to go just to be with him, when actually it was to monitor the spending of our valuable cash. He wouldn't hear of it. I was to just rest, read, and relax, and he would be back soon.   T w o hours later, I was still sitting in front of the window, waiting. How many bags could one meal possibly occupy? Six, I found out later, and all but $9.11 of our cash.

Two more hours, and I was ready to chew my own arm off and eat it. I was starved.

Pretending I had to potty, I silently passed through the living room just in time to see my groom, who was leaning over a fire in the fireplace, drop pieces of raw chicken down into the flame. The fat on the skin emitted a terrible snapping sound, and the smell made me nauseous.

"Oh, no," he muttered quietly while reaching into the flames with a long meat fork and pulled the chicken parts out to safety.

I'm probably going to die, I thought, throwing myself across the bed.

Another hour and the dinner call came. The little kitchen table— and I use the word *kitchen* loosely—was elegantly set with candles, tin dishes (those blue kind with white speckles), mismatched silverware, and carefully folded napkins (his precious, linen preaching handkerchiefs).

He gingerly seated me, then himself, and proceeded to pour red Kool-Aid into jelly jar glasses. Then came the blessing.

While he blessed, I looked. *Oh, gross! Brown rice!* I am a southern girl, and southern girls eat only one kind of rice: white with cholesterol-inducing, artery-clogging, brown fat gravy. This rice was brown and very dry. Then came the vegetable from hell—Brussels sprouts, little tiny heads rolling around in your mouth. In my opinion, they are the gagging vegetable. They are the ones with which your mom threatened to keep you ten years at the table unless you ate every one. Then there was the chicken, blackened before that method was ever popular.

My sweetheart served me up generous portions of *everything*.

Dear God, help me, I silently prayed before I cut open my burned sacrifice. It ran red and pink blood. That was it. For the entire meal I employed my years of training as a preacher's kid. I cut, moved food around my plate, raised the fork halfway to my mouth, and bantered witty repartee without actually eating anything.

He noticed. "Why aren't you eating?"

Did I dare start my marriage on a lie?

Setting down the fork with only two tines and the dull mismatched knife, I looked into the eyes of my beloved husband of seven days, my soul mate, my high priest . . . do you get the idea? (Please know that I was twenty-one years old and knew everything.)

"I hate chicken, but I hate this chicken even more than usual. It has salmonella spores waiting to kill me. This rice is dry and tasteless, and you forgot to make the gravy. The vegetable, Brussels sprouts, is my worst, most dreaded vegetable of all time. Tonight I'll have dreams that a large burned chicken dressed up as a Brussels sprout with brown rice under its wings is chasing me."

I think he got the point. Randi was totally silent. Only then did I see the tears, big old silent tears sliding out of those baby blues down his cheeks. I had hurt him. He was barely breathing.

When he did speak, he was scarcely audible: "All I wanted to do was bless you. Chicken, Brussels sprouts, and brown rice are my favorite meal."

To this I answered, "Well, honey, if you wanted to bless me, why didn't you find out what *my* favorite meal was?"

Please don't judge me too harshly. I could say I was raised in the jungle by monkeys, but no, that wasn't me. Okay, I was the daughter of a poor sharecropper from Alamalooa. No, not me either. Just go ahead and say it: young and dumb. But bright and truthful. Neither of us saw the situation through the other's eyes.

The next week, when I was deep into my hour of prayer, I got to the part where I recited how much I love my Lord. Then came the litany of all that I had been doing for Him and His kingdom. I thought, *This is the part where He now thanks me and tells me how much He loves and appreciates me.* But I was no longer just the child; I was a woman of God, a pastor's wife. I had a husband and a new congregation to care for. I waited . . . Silence.

"Lord?" My voice sounded like a five-year-old's.

Did you desire to please Me with all those works? He asked. I had never heard my heavenly Father sound quite like that.

"Yes, my precious Lord."

Then you should have found out what I like, beloved.

It was my turn to be silent, my turn to be unable to stop the stinging tears from streaming down my face. But suddenly I understood.

If we spend our lives giving Him chicken, brown rice, and Brussels sprouts when He wants a filet, baked potato, and corn, we have wasted our lives.

We Must Give Him What He Wants

What pleases God is growing in patience. He looks for that. We somehow believe that praying, fasting, and tithing are the ultimate "God pleasers." Even though these things draw us close to Him, the end desire is patience. According to His Word, patience ranks high on the list of character traits that God desires to cultivate in us. I suppose when patience is working in our lives, we are able to suffer many things without "turning" on God. Our spirits remain sweet; our words encouraging. "Look how she trusts God" would be the greatest compliment we could receive. "Look how her God loves her" will be the highest compliment spoken in reply.

And while you're being patient, you might want to try a little cheesecake for comfort. You might be surprised at how many properties of healing cheesecake contains. On many a dark night just one piece of cheesecake had the power to lift off incredible sorrow. Well, at least temporarily. Three days later, after I come to my senses, I think, *Cathy, what have you done?* When I finally remember the first piece I ate, I always wonder who ate the other six slices.

As James admonished in his book, "Let patience have its perfect work, that you may be perfect and complete, lacking nothing" (1:4).

Chapter Four

If God Lived with These People, I'd Get a Bigger Reward

In this chapter I want to say a few words "about words" to the women who are involved in ministry. The greatest thing about the ministry is the people. The worst thing about the ministry is the people. People are like elevators. They'll take you up when you do something they like, or they'll take you down when you disappoint them.

I describe the ministry with this lively analogy. It's like putting your head on the chopping block, someone cutting it off "in love," and Jesus healing you. You then lay it back down, only to have someone else chop it off again, and again Jesus heals it. Then you . . . Oh, well, I think you get the picture.

A young man confided in me that he couldn't wait to go into the ministry so that he wouldn't have to work. Fifteen minutes later as I lay on the floor doubled over in laughter, the man still didn't have a clue about what he had said to set me off like that.

It is no accident that it is called "the work of the ministry." Let me remind you that your words are tools of the ministry. Spoken in haste or anger, they will do harm to you and wound others. Words have incredible potential for good or ill. James mentioned that it is possible to bless God and curse others with the same mouth. He said that no spring should be pouring out both sweet and brackish water.

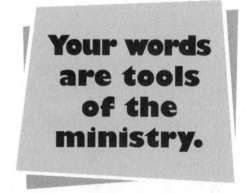

Your words are tools of the ministry.

Wow! Words are powerful ambassadors, indeed. Prideful words, stubbornly maintained, can even make enemies out of the very people who love us the most. That is not the heartbeat of the Father. I think that some people in ministry actually believe their entire calling is to tell others what to do and how to do it. How they got that perspective remains a mystery to me.

Parting Is Such Sweet Sorrow

Over the course of a life of service, people leave jobs and responsibilities to go on to other opportunities. Unfortunately some folks seem to feel that the way they left their last employer and the people associated with that position will have no bearing on their new situation.

Dear reader, let me gently tell you that this is not so. The way you leave your last position is the way you will enter the next one.

In other words, if you leave a job with unkind words in the air and go on to another position, you will find that the dirty laundry will tend to follow you, and it will affect your new job situation and relationships.

Did you walk out of that last church because of misunderstandings and you now have a wounded spirit? Your reputation as a troublemaker or a malcontent will follow you to the new church. Maybe you just slipped out the back door, and because it was a large congregation, you assumed you would not be missed. Wrong! Leaving one place and going to another is never simple.

Now I will have to admit, I hate confrontation. I'm so mercy motivated that I apologize for everything. But if I'm going to be wrong, let it be on the side of mercy.

"But, Cathy, you said your past doesn't determine your future."

> ## If I'm going to be wrong, let it be on the side of mercy.

That's still true, but it doesn't give you a license to go around with a trail of broken relationships. It's hard to apologize. It's also very humbling, but it begins a healing process. You have chosen the high road for excellence. Are you willing to pay the price?

Not everyone desires to be reconciled to us. I am a Pollyanna. I want everyone to love each other, be nice, have no problems; however, that is an unrealistic expectation.

A woman in our ministry desperately wanted to be involved in the activity of our church. But it wasn't long before we heard murmuring and grumbling surrounding a problem.

Upon investigation, we found that this woman's name always came up in the conversation. There would be a controversy, and she was at the root of every situation. Little problems always revolved around her wherever she went. She wasn't an evil woman. She wasn't a Jezebel or even a rebel. She just could not exercise spiritual maturity in relationships.

Some wonderful Christians out there have incredible gifting and talents, but their inability to walk with others disqualifies them from all but the simplest services. She was such a woman—disqualified because of her inability to get along with others.

Of course, it was my responsibility to bring instruction to this saint. Have you ever tried to bring correction to someone who

(a) never, ever believes she is capable of doing anything wrong;

(b) begins to cry, saying that she has only tried to be a blessing, and that the enemy is just lying about her;

(c) somehow makes it *your* fault, causing you to end up apologizing for the next half hour; then finally

(d) deeply hurt, forgives you, accepting *your* apology, then leaves, promising to pray for you and *your* problem?

I then began looking through the want ads to see if there were any jobs available for ice fishermen at the South Pole.

Yes, we can run away to the South Pole, but I have it on good authority that there is a church member at the South Pole Assembly of God by the name of Aunt Arctica. She was in charge of the church whale blubber potluck. Well, it's an ugly story, but I'll repeat it so you can pray.

After the potluck was over on Wednesday night, she filled up twelve baskets of leftover blubber and took them home to her husband, Sloan. Unbelievable!

Though we *are* called to love others, I don't have time to spend on people who are going to pull me down or on well-meaning Christians who are going to subtract from me. These are the ones who have some sort of controversy continually surrounding them.

That doesn't make me a bad person. It doesn't mean that I have no love for others, but I am not called to be by their side twenty-four hours a day, seven days a week. There are some you lovingly hold at arm's length and say, "I care about you, but I'm going higher." They enjoy dissension, misery, and pity parties. Let them sit there in self-pity.

I know, it's much easier said than done, especially if you are a mercy-motivated soul or if you shy away from confrontation. I hated rejection in any form so much that I dreaded anything that would force me into a face-off. I used to have to really get angry and tired of being used or lied about and pushed around. Then I'd just turn on the next one who "pushed my button." Imagine the person's surprise when the kind, sweet pastor's wife and mentor turned into a spiritual Mr. Hyde.

Oh, the lessons we have to learn as we strive to be women of God who are committed to being the best we can be in His service. As for me, to stay on my good side, remember never to start your conversation with "I just want to tell you this in love . . ." and you'll be okay.

Ministry (and Charity) Begins at Home

This issue about speaking truth with love, about carefully using our tongues and respecting and valuing others with our words, is very important among our families. One day, after a particularly intense, shall we say, disagreement, my husband and I were still at an impasse. The problem as I saw it was that I, of course, was right. He just couldn't admit it.

I thought if I continued talking, eventually he would see the folly of his ways and come around to my extremely right point of view. In reality, all I managed to do was to make him angrier. I'm sure, being very spiritual, you have never experienced anything like this.

The Holy Spirit continued to whisper in my ear, *Okay, Cathy. Now be quiet.*

Just a minute, sweet Dove of Heaven. I had just had another brilliant thought. *Let me make just one more point and then I'll shut up.* My point started out something like this: "Well, do you remember eighteen years ago when you . . . ," which only reminded him of something else to say in angry defense.

Again the Holy Spirit pleaded, *Now, stop! This is wrong.*

But by then it had gone too far.

Randi spun around, pointing his finger at me, and exclaimed, "You make me so mad! No one else gets my goat like you!"

"Well, that just proves you have a goat to get, and God's going to separate the sheep from the goats." *Wow*, I thought, *that was excellent!*

I had managed to verbally smack him around and use the Scripture to drive home a spiritual principle. *Now, Holy Spirit, what were You saying?*

I learned a terrible, valuable lesson that day. No, not that I had bettered my husband in an argument. I learned that I could be right in principle and end up being wrong—very wrong.

The point of this chapter is this: whether you are a full-time minister or one whose ministry is between the walls of your home, there's a right way and a wrong way to do and say all things. Let your words be "seasoned with salt" (Col. 4:6 NIV) and your deeds be done "as unto the Lord," and your ministry will be one of excellence!

It sure beats being the Women's Ministry president of the South Pole Assembly!

In the next chapter I want to share with you the importance of being ready to lay down your dreams when they don't match the ones that God (or your family) has for you and the ministry.

Chapter Five

Straight Hair in a Permed World

One of my eight-year-old children (I have three that age) came home from school today and announced in front of my prayer group that she is an alcoholic. Can you imagine what must have gone through the minds of those holy ladies? Let's see, how can I describe what happened next?

Okay, have you ever seen the look on your husband's face when your pastor and his wife are having dinner in your home and the poodle carries a pair of your husband's dirty underwear into the dining room?

No? Trust me. It's a pretty horrible picture . . . the underwear, your pastor, his dainty, proper wife. Talk about no air in the room! No one breathed, not even the poodle. Your husband then says something like: "Gee, honey, did the boys leave their whitey tighties on the floor again?" My boys wear a seven slim. My husband doesn't.

It turned out that my daughter is not an alcoholic after all. But before the particulars became known, eight very serious intercessors began binding her to deliver her out of the clutches of drink.

It seems that her school (private but not religious) had launched an Alcohol Awareness Week. All my child heard was "drink" and answered yes, of course, her mom and dad drink.

I am so glad that I read the flyer that gave me a heads-up on Thursday, Heroin Day. Had Hannah and I not had our "little talk," she would have said she has a *heroine*, and it would have been me, her mother.

Having children has totally bent all my life's rules. Oh, those vows that I made as an eighteen-year-old baby-sitter: "I'll tell you what! My kids will *never* eat sugar," and "Can you believe she allowed her five-year-old to fix her own hair and go out in public?" I had a litany of complaints about the mothers and their children that I sat for, and I made general observations based on my unique ability to criticize everyone.

It goes without saying that my children are stunning examples of model behavior. They never leave the house unless their hair is perfectly coifed. They wear matching designer outfits, neatly pressed shorts and knee socks for my boys, Laura Ashley with white tights and Capezio shoes for the girls. And all liars shall have their place in the lake of fire where they will burn forever and ever alongside the horrible children they baby-sat.

My Name Is Cathy Kennedy

I was in the third grade when President Kennedy was assassinated. The only significant things I can remember are getting a day off from school and seeing the matching blue his-and-her Chesterfield coats that Caroline and John-John wore. I remember well that Caroline always had her hair pulled back and fastened by a bow and John-John had a bowl haircut. I would stare forever at their picture. The politics were lost on me. I didn't care. I do remember my southern Republican father saying, "Those Kennedys," followed by something unintelligible.

Oh, how I wanted to be Caroline Kennedy! My mother and daddy were Assembly of God pastors, and they would never buy us matching blue Chesterfield coats. They thought John-John's hair was way too long, and besides that, Daddy buzzed the boys' hair every summer with his home barbershop set from Sears. There would be no Caroline hair for me because when one is blessed with one's deceased Aunt Minnie's fine, stringy hair, one gets it cut, followed by a pink Lilly permanent wave.

It wasn't too late for my children. Their destiny was yet to be formed. I practiced with my dolls. I would marry an Irish tenor. We would name our sons Sean, Patrick, Ryan, and Flynn. Our daughters would have more trendy names, like Heather and Jennifer. They would all wear matching blue Chesterfield coats, and the boys would have John-John bowl haircuts to make the most of their lustrous brown hair.

Thanksgiving would find us sitting around the long, elegantly set dining table. As the boys saw me enter the room, dressed in a pink-and-white-checked shirtwaist dress, crisp white linen apron, pearls, and pillbox hat, their little blue eyes would glisten.

"Mother," little Flynn would say with delight, "you're so beautiful. Isn't she, Papa?"

My gorgeous husband, Joe Feeney, would try to grab and kiss

my neck, and the little girls would giggle. "Only the most beauti-ful lass in or out of Ireland," he would gently whisper in my ear.

"Oh, Joe, the turkey." After all, I would serve the most mag-nificent twenty-five-pound tom turkey, done to a golden brown, stuffing spilling out onto the gleaming Wedgwood platter. The room would smell like fresh cranberries. Then little Patrick, his cherubic face looking up at me, would utter his very first words: "I want some turkey, please. God is so faithful. God bless us, every one!"

We would all clap, the children squealing with delight. Papa Joe, clearing his throat, would then ask us to bow in prayer singing "We Gather Together," the traditional holiday hymn. As Joe joined in, his rich tenor voice would cause my heart to skip a beat. We would be the envy of everyone.

You know the passage in Psalms that says God sits in the heav-ens and laughs? Well, I think I know what He is laughing at.

My dream, my desire for the life I wanted as a seven-year-old, was not evil. It wasn't even misguided. I just didn't have the advan-tage of seeing my life from God's point of view.

It still absolutely amazes me that the Father takes the trouble to lead us, push us and, if we still don't have a clue, shove us toward our great destiny.

God's Dream

My barrel-chested Irish tenor husband, Joe, with the dancing eyes turned out to be a twenty-eight-year-old Jew who, though filled with barrels of enthusiasm, can't carry a tune in a bucket. Pregnant with our first child, I cried for days when Joe—I mean Randi—said he didn't think God wanted us to name our son Patrick O'Shea Limerick Lechner.

He was, after all, rabbi and spiritual leader of Temple Aron Kodesh, a messianic Jewish synagogue in Fort Lauderdale.

We settled on Joshua. I might not call him Paddy, but I could still put him in a blue Chesterfield coat and brown shoes and give him a bowl haircut. Who cares if it was 105 degrees?

Then God allows the death of *your* dream, a little bit at a time, while revealing *His* dream so that you really begin to see how merciful He is when He didn't give you what you thought you couldn't live without.

The day our Jerusha Rose was born changed our lives forever. *Jerusha* in Hebrew means "the Lord's inheritance." The biblical Queen Jerusha gave birth to kings and was a righteous woman. Our Jerusha is now an exquisite twenty-four-year-old young woman. She is gifted musically, plays the piano, and sings like an angel. Her path has led her to Christian International School of Ministry where she is preparing herself to follow the call of God into full-time ministry with a husband she is fervently believing God to bring in. I told her to

> God allows the death of your dream, a little bit at a time, while revealing His dream.

check out Ireland because I still have this little blue Chesterfield coat.

"That's your dream, Mom, not mine. My kids, if I have any, are going to wear Calvin Klein and Tommy Hilfiger."

My next children don't look like the Kennedys either. My eight-year-old daughter Hannah (remember the former alcoholic?) is African-American. Asking her to wear a dress is tantamount to child abuse in her opinion. She loves baggy shirts, overalls, sports pants, and Skecher sneakers. She wept at our last family Christmas picture when I made her wear a red velvet sweater. "I look like an idiot," sobbed this five-and-a-half-foot, 120-pound eight-year-old.

All Dressed Up but Not Ready to Go

Once, I found these red-and-white gingham mother-and-son matching outfits in a specialty catalog. The one-piece boy's overalls were even called "John-Johns" after you-know-who. They were above the knee and had smocking across the front with little geese and dogs. They came with white knee socks and adorable white shirts that had rounded Peter Pan collars. My credit card practically fell out of my wallet dancing with glee, insisting on purchasing the outfits.

The day the clothes arrived, I carefully pressed them and ignored my four-year-old son when he asked me, "Whose ugly dress is that?" I had bought the entire family matching red-gingham outfits.

It is always a special event in the Lechner house when a child's adoption becomes final. We always fly the entire family to the county courthouse for what is a momentous day.

We might not be Kennedys, but we would sure look like them.

One by one the children put on their smocked gingham outfits.

The little girls wore white ankle socks with delicate lace and black patent Mary Janes. The boys, dressed and ready to go except for their hair, stood looking silently forlorn with pleading little eyes staring up at me.

Samuel Josiah and Gabriel Levi are not twins, but were then both four years old. They have white biological mothers and African-American biological fathers. Therefore, it doesn't matter how much gel, mousse, straightener, or hair spray I use, their hair does only two things: curl up and then poof out. There would be no John-John hair in my life—ever. My dad remembered that he still had that electric barber set from Sears if I wanted him to cut their hair. "Best $9.99 I ever spent. Those fancy salons will charge you that much just for one haircut."

My husband was on his way out the front door when he suddenly stopped in his tracks. "What in the name of—Cathy, what do my boys have on?"

Jerusha, who was twenty at the time, started giggling. In a barely audible singsongy voice, she said, "I told you so."

Briefly I tried to explain the certain sophistication and elegance of the John-John suit to my husband. I will now tell you that, to my utter dismay (and not that I haven't tried), he has no sense of fashion!

"Rich people have dressed their children in these for years. Princess Diana still puts William and Harry in them for Christmas photos," I reasoned.

"Princess Diana is dead. The boys look like sissies," and he started to unbutton the Peter Pan collar.

"Well, *my* boys look traditional and classic. Besides, it's too late to change them. We'll miss the plane, and the girls and I all match them!" I knew then how Jackie might have felt from time to time.

Just then my mother and dad arrived. "Is *that* what they're wearing? They look like Little Lord Fauntleroy," my mom exclaimed. "They look like sissies."

"Aha! Aha!" my husband piped up. He knew he had me. Both my parents agreed with him. Now, in my twenty-five years of marriage, my mother has never agreed with my husband, not out of spite, but because she is usually right. Of all days. This woman who dressed *her* son in a Deputy Dawg and Huckleberry Hound sweatshirt suddenly agreed with my husband.

Ten minutes later, to the great relief of two little boys, a husband, and a grandmother who thought her daughter had temporarily lost her mind, we were out the door. My little gingham dream was cast off, lying on the floor, with the poodle curled up on top of it. I refuse to give those little suits away. They still hang in my boys' closet as a reminder that dreams change.

So I have two little curly-headed boys who are eight and make their dad and me laugh; a three-year-old who wears her brother's camouflage pajamas to Wal-Mart; a six-year-old and a four-year-old who love bright red lipstick, have huge bows perched on top of their fuzzy heads, and possess a passion for sugar that must be from the Twilight Zone; and of course, our eight-year-old African-American who is *not* an alcoholic!

Understand the Source of Your Dream

I overheard our teenage baby-sitter telling her girlfriend, "My children are never going to eat sugar. And what's with her letting that girl wear her brother's pajamas?"

I just laughed. I need to remember to pray for her. She'll probably become a nun! Joking aside, dreams are important in life. Expectations can be powerful agents of blessing, or they can hinder and harm our lives. Some dreams are the basic ingredients for laughter and great family memories. Others, unless yielded to God, can become burdensome and cause those of us who cling to them heartache and often heartburn.

> **Expectations can be powerful agents of blessing.**

Dear reader, unless you are fully convinced your dream originated with God and it is His clearly defined purpose for you to see it fulfilled, release that dream when it is clear there is no valid reason for you to hold on to it. Be free!

This idea of being free is the thrust of our next chapter. I have found that being free to be "me" is the key to dealing with the deadly disease of inadequacy. Read on.

Chapter Six

Nobody Understands!

As we go through life, all of us in one way or another are challenged. And in my opinion, one of the major hurdles for women determined to fulfill their unique calling from God is the awful, life-destroying feeling of inadequacy. This deadly virus can infect and affect all areas of our lives. Look at my experience for a moment.

In my particular world, I meet thousands of people. I never get an opportunity to connect with most of them. Some become dear friends, and God uses them to pour into my life.

I am married, I have seven children (six of whom are under the age of eight), and I travel fifty weekends out of the year. Because of my lifestyle, there are not too many people who can relate to me.

If I don't guard my heart, I fall into the I'm-the-only-person-on-the-planet-who-has-ever-faced-this-problem syndrome. In reality, it's not so.

I have had the great joy of knowing many people all over the world. Although the details of our lives may be different, we experience and face the same situations. Because of this, we have the ability to encourage others. Please be aware that these experiences come with a hefty price tag. We are told in Proverbs: "My son [or daughter], be attentive to my Wisdom [godly Wisdom learned by actual and costly experience]" (5:1 AMP).

At my meetings when I sell books to attendees, I sign as many as I can. People seem to enjoy having a book signed by the author. As I sign my name, the question that goes through my mind is, *Do they realize the price I have paid with my life, my soul, and my pride so I can share these experiences with them?*

We are surrounded by thousands of great books, written by great men and women of God. When I read a page from *The Hiding Place* by Corrie Ten Boom, I weep. Nicky Cruz's life story affected and changed my life. I have come to the realization that these writers have probably been to hell and back. They have learned life's lessons by actual and costly experience.

I have found that I as the reader am the blessed one. If you are like me, there is usually one paragraph in a book that especially touches your life. If we take the written truth and apply it to our lives, it may just save us from a trip to hell and back.

What You See Is What You Get

My heart's desire is to share truth from my life and perspective. The most common encouragement that I receive from my peers attests to the fact that I am "real." What you see is what you get.

That, my friend, gives hope to others. God really does use ordinary people.

Women and men say how good it is to know they are not alone. I try to be transparent about both my failures and my successes. Transparency is good as long as it produces answers, and it is a powerful tool from a place of victory. So let me tell you today that one of my biggest struggles has been with the enemy called "inadequacy."

Facing challenges is just a part of life. (Notice I didn't use the word *problem*. I found out the hard way that the word deeply offends the there-is-no-problem people. I think they're from Pluto.) Our inability to look at and overcome these issues makes life difficult.

"I Just Can't Do It"

Frankly we are all inadequate if we are honest, except, of course, the ones from Pluto, who have no problems.

I have often cried out to God, "I can't! You've got the wrong girl. I'm overwhelmed." Your inability is not a major problem to God. But your remaining inadequate causes a problem. The dictionary's meaning of *inadequate* is "insufficient." You can probably guess where I am going with this.

As a little girl, I was amazed by Bible heroes. Their stories were as real to me as my own. I'll admit, I was a bit strange, but I would read and reread the stories about David, Abigail, Sarah, and Miriam as though I didn't know the outcome. When we look at the Bible heroes we think are so godly, so amazing, they seem adequate in everything they did.

Wrong! They were human—just as we are. They faced insecurity, inferiority, fear, and rejection, and they dealt with their own inadequacy. Their stories included everything from neglect, loss, and misunderstanding to abandonment. Their remarkable lives, which we read about in the Bible today, are no more significant than ours. God just chose to position them early on in His story, and He made them heroes by recording their experiences as examples.

History Makers of the Present

Guess what? You and I are history makers today. Paul compared the Christian to an "epistle [letter] . . . known and read by all men" (2 Cor. 3:2). We are reminded to be examples to our own generation by Paul's words to Timothy in 1 Timothy 4.

If you and I don't rise up and get in our appointed places at our appointed times, then who will? Despite his successes and failures, King David "served God's purpose in his own generation" (Acts 13:36 NIV).

> **You and I are history makers today.**

We seriously need that same gut resolve if we are going to rescue the multitudes who are every minute of every day falling into a lost eternity.

God Is a Nothing Maker

When I started out ministering, I was following in the long shadow of my immensely anointed, phenomenally gifted preacher husband.

People would sit spellbound as he, the associate pastor, opened the Word in the most incredible way. He knew all the Greek and Hebrew. Then he would begin to flow in the Word of knowledge while praying for people. Miracles were common. I kept to myself at the piano, softly playing ooh-ah music in the background.

There was an exception, when the pastor's wife asked me to speak to the ladies on a Saturday afternoon. She figured such a gifted man of God just *had* to be married to an equally anointed teacher and preacher.

Well, she figured wrong.

My husband answered for me. "Yes, Sister Thistletoe, she'll be glad to minister."

I wanted *him* dead, and then I wanted *me* dead. Since neither of us fell to the floor, I had to weakly respond, "Okay, but I must tell you, I'm not as good as . . ."

My husband jabbed me in the back with his elbow. "She's so modest. My wife is excellent. You should hear her at home!" Then it was my turn to jab.

I fully prepared twenty-five pages of notes, and I stayed up all Friday night praying. I thought that was what you were supposed to do.

The next morning, I was on after the coffee and donuts. Coffee and donuts speed up your metabolism, but then the rush of sugar drops you and you fall asleep.

I preached my twenty-five pages of notes in ten minutes and still managed to put two women to sleep. My talk was boring. I think one woman pinched her kid so he'd cry and she could leave. *Never again*, I thought. *I will never again try to minister*. That was about twenty-two years ago.

No Problem to God

Remember that our being inadequate is not a problem to God. He loves to mold awesome things out of what seems like nothing. The problem is our choosing to remain inadequate.

Looking back now, I can see the steps God took me through to make me into a woman with a message to share. I stopped trying to be somebody I was not.

I admire many incredible and gifted teachers in the body of Christ. I began to listen to those men and women, and when they spoke, I could hear God through them. When Women Aglow International called me shortly after my first miserable endeavor to speak at a local meeting, I accepted. Instead of trying to teach some really deep message on stuff that I didn't understand, I chose to talk about my personal struggles and how God brought me through them.

Only one person nodded off. I began to see how the simplicity of the gospel brought better results than my knowledge (or lack of knowledge) of the Rapture. Soon I was speaking once a month to small groups of women. That became twice a month, and now I travel to speaking engagements between forty-five and fifty weekends per year all over the world. I have had the honor of speaking before hundreds as well as thousands. The message does not change much. I simply share what I have learned in marriage and motherhood.

Your life experiences that have ended in victory are your testimony, and as long as your heart is beating, you are a candidate for a miracle. Precious one, you have a lifetime ahead of you to try again. Whether you are just beginning your journey, or are closer to the end of it, there is always hope.

We must stop saying, "I can't," and fill our mouths with, "I can and I will." Our willingness to step out beyond our fear, insecurity, and inadequacy just might bring needed light and life to someone's very painful existence.

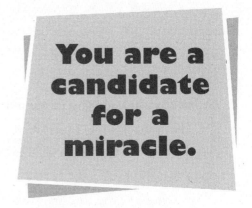

You are a candidate for a miracle.

Starting Out in the School of the Spirit

In our very first pastorate, we were blessed to have an incredible couple serving as associate ministers. The husband was a college professor, and his wife had a master's degree in Spanish history and language. Both taught at the nearby university. The wife had taught herself to play the keyboard, make banners, cook phenomenal all-natural meals, and cut her own hair.

It wasn't her fault that the people in our congregation naturally sought her out for counseling or ministry, for every potluck, and for service on the worship team. She was older, smarter, and thinner than I was—and immensely talented. The only thing I could do was sing and play the piano, but because it was a messianic Jewish synagogue, I didn't know any of the music.

One dear sister asked me if I would be playing for the Jewish Feast of Passover. I was twenty-one with a baby on the way and sick as a dog. I could only weakly answer, "No." I was really thinking, but afraid to admit it, *No, I don't know how to play those songs. I don't know how to prepare matzo ball soup. I'm useless. I'm a failure.*

The reason I used to say, "I can't," was, to a degree, that I really couldn't. I was starting out in the school of life and the school of the Spirit. How can you give away something that is not yet in you?

"Devote yourself to . . . reading . . . to preaching and to teaching" (1 Tim. 4:13 NIV). Perhaps right now you can't do certain things, but verse 15 urges, "Practice and cultivate and meditate upon these duties" (AMP).

Speaking of practice, that's exactly what I did on the piano. To build confidence in playing the music that was so new to me, I bought a Jewish songbook and practiced until I felt my playing was passable if everyone screamed out the Hebrew words.

> **Our challenge is to start growing out of our inabilities.**

I also practiced cooking. Now I can make the best lox, bagel, and cream cheese plate, and even my Jewish husband says my matzo ball soup tastes like his grandmother's. Of course, she's dead, so the competition is not as great.

If something becomes a priority in our lives, it is amazing how we can make it happen.

We all feel inadequate until we start to grow. Our challenge is to start growing out of our inabilities. By responding to challenges, we will feel less inclined to say, "I can't."

Be encouraged, and determine to grow in your understanding of your Father's ability to guide you into your full potential. When you seek to actively reach your potential for God, you will face hindrances that may frustrate your attempts to live out your dream. In the next chapter, we are going to look more closely at this situation.

Chapter Seven

Your Story Will Never Be Average

$\int$ ince the day I met Christ at about the age of twelve, I have never ceased to love Him. For me to backslide and break His heart is an absolute abhorrent thought.

But I will be honest with you. There have been times when life was screaming for my attention, and I neglected to grow spiritually. I would wait until nighttime to open my Bible, then read one verse and wake up the next morning with the light on and my Bible on my belly.

Even the ministry competed for my time with the Lord.

I was busy trying to raise my children, make sure homework got done, and prepare decent meals. Then there was the "tired" factor. I was always tired, sad, and basically a grumbling person.

The consequences were that I had sowed a famine in my life. I never meant to; it just happened.

Sowing a Famine

Beloved, if you sow a famine in your life, don't be surprised that you feel disabled and inadequate. When I realized this, I chose to change. God didn't punish me. Instead, He promised to redeem the time and to restore the lost opportunity. Isn't that wonderful?

> **He promised to redeem the time and to restore the lost opportunity.**

I see a couple every week in church with their children. Up and down, in and out. While it is commendable that they bring their children to church, they never get anything from the sermon because they spend the entire service in the hallway talking to someone. They refuse to put their children in the nursery or kids' church, so neither of them receives anything. They are unknowingly sowing to themselves a famine.

Ministers (gulp!) can also, without realizing it, sow famine. They fail to position themselves for growth, and then eventually find that they have nothing substantial to give.

Growth is such a critical aspect of our destiny that we must learn to confront and overcome any challenges in our lives that would hinder our growth.

Paul encouraged us, "Therefore, my dear ones . . . work out—cultivate, carry out to the goal, and fully complete—your own salvation with reverence and awe and trembling" (Phil. 2:12 AMP).

At one time I became involved in deliverance ministry, and it almost destroyed me. No, not the demonic powers that manifested themselves in the lives of my church members. They, I think, I could have handled. What almost did me in was the sheer exhaustion from working with people like one very precious young woman who had a standing appointment with me every Wednesday morning for deliverance. In my pitiful immaturity, I sat week after week after week listening to tales of abuse, rejection, fear, and perversion. Week after week I would seat her in my office and begin to pray.

By the end of an hour she was elated. She would grab her purse, smile sweetly, give a little wave, and say, "See ya next week." But when she left, I looked as though a train had run over me. In fact, come to think of it, I probably looked as if *I* was the one who needed deliverance. My voice was shot from yelling at the devil to let her go. Distraught, disheveled, and disheartened, I laid my head on my desk in despair.

I now owed my baby-sitter thirty dollars, and once again the young woman had "forgotten" her checkbook. That made it about two years of forgetting the checkbook.

Rebuking myself, I suddenly heard the Holy Spirit say, *You are not helping her.* I figured it was the voice of some lying demon that the woman had accidentally left behind in my office. He continued, *She wants* Me *to do everything for her, and I won't. Now she wants* you *to do everything for her, and you are. You are the only one who is growing.*

You know how God can say a thousand things in a moment? My spiritual eyes were opened, and in an instant I understood. This woman seldom came to church and never served the body in any capacity. Too often Christians want God to do it all for them. They want to show up at any time and expect—no, demand—attention without being an active participant in their own deliverance or pro-

God expects us to be actively pursuing our destiny goals.

vision. But according to Paul's words in Philippians 2:12, God expects *us* to be actively pursuing our destiny goals.

"God, why didn't You show me this sooner?" But I knew the answer. Having the young woman need me inflated my pride. I could tell people I had a full schedule of appointments. I was unwittingly enabling her and others to look to me to change them. Lasting change comes only from the Spirit of God, changing you from the inside.

I Gotta Get Out of Here!

Our twenty-four-year-old daughter, Jerusha, is absolutely and without a doubt the most generous, talented, gracious, and lovely young woman I know.

She remained at home to attend a local college in order to help me with all the little babies we adopted. She sacrificed a social life because we needed help in the evenings with dinner, homework, and baths. I never heard her complain to me or to her friends about our expectations for her.

We were so grateful for her hard work, her service to the family and ministry, that we made sure she had what she needed financially. We made $465 monthly car payments, bought auto insurance, and provided free room and board, pocket money, and a Visa card.

Because she never had to pay the bills, and because she didn't really ask for much, I never said anything when she bought stuff that wasn't on the grocery list. The day I sent her to the mall with my American Express card to pick up a gift certificate, she found herself a pair of shoes, a necklace, and some earrings. Again, I said nothing.

When my husband addressed the situation, he was met by my bewilderment.

"You're not helping her, Cathy," he said. I immediately began my defense by recounting how much she sacrificed. He responded, "Honey, you just feel guilty, but your way is not helping her."

You know the saying, "The truth hurts"? Wow! It felt like an arrow hitting my heart. He was right. *Now, how can I stop these tears and get out of the room without letting him know how right he is?* I thought.

I wanted to lash out in anger and tell him he didn't understand because she and I were so close. *That's it,* I thought. I accused him of being jealous and unfair, and I told him that he just plain didn't understand.

By that time I was sobbing. He put his big ol' arms around me and pulled me close. He was gentle and kind, and when he spoke, there were no words of hurt and bitterness. Only tenderness. Gently he explained it was God's timing. Our daughter, my best friend, needed to pursue her own destiny.

That night I slipped into her bedroom as I had for twenty-four years and sat down beside her. "Scoot over, babe," I almost whispered.

"Mommy, are you crying?" she asked as she moved to make room for me.

"Jerusha, tell me the truth. Don't spare my feelings. Do you want to leave home?" Holding my breath, I waited. It took her about two seconds to reply.

"Mom, I've gotta get out of here. I love you and Dad and the kids, but if I don't go now, I'll be trapped forever. Is it okay?" At that moment, she still looked seven.

Yeah, it was okay. The next month she left for Bible college and is in hot pursuit of her dream.

She called me at the end of the first week to apprise me of her new life, which included grocery shopping for her first apartment. She had gone to Wal-Mart because then she wouldn't have to "waste gas going to two different stores." I chuckled.

I encouraged her to stick to the diet (sorry, it's called genetic nagging, and it's not my fault) that we had begun before she left. "Get some of those Weight Watcher meals," I advised her.

"Mother, Lean Cuisines are the exact same thing, and they are eleven cents cheaper. I saved a dollar and fourteen cents with my coupons," she announced with incredible pride.

Eleven cents? Coupons? She was the child who one week earlier used my credit card to buy a Big Mac.

I never realized that she loved me so much she couldn't stand the thought of breaking my heart. Jerusha was living her life to serve my dream and my destiny.

Perhaps you, too, are serving another person's dreams. Many folks are. But when it becomes easier to serve someone else's dream than to step out for your own, it's time to put a demand on your faith.

On Reading the Word

It is staggering how many Christians do not read the Word of God regularly. Satan (our adversary, who has the desire to steal your potential and make you feel hopeless) will do everything possible to prevent you from getting into the Word. But the Word of God has the power to change, renew, equip, and enable you.

While at a conference one weekend, I asked the women, about two thousand in attendance, how many of them did not like themselves. I could not believe how many hands went up in that auditorium—beautiful, young, and successful women who did not like themselves.

We all go through places of being dissatisfied with what we see. I loathe my voice on teaching tapes; I cringe when I see myself on television.

I was being interviewed on a popular Christian television program one night. It was a Johnny Carson sort of format with me sitting on the couch and the host in a chair at an angle to my left.

He asked me a very serious and personal question, and as I started to answer, he gave the cameraman a signal to take the camera off both of us and put it on me.

To my horror, he began to primp, fixing his abnormal hair in the floor monitor, not paying one bit of attention to a thing I was saying. There must be a balance somewhere between self-loathing and self-hair worship.

If you don't like the way you are, it's okay. The Word of God is not just a concept to change you. Seriously get into the Word and it will change you.

Do you want to be set free from the old? The Word promises to renew. Everything in life is deteriorating, but God's Word has the supernatural ability to take you in the opposite direction.

I try to walk two to five miles every day. It's not all that much, but it makes me feel that I'm doing something to stave off flabby fat that keeps plotting to overtake me at night.

My mom gave me some family pictures, and in them was a black-and-white of my ninety-four-year-old grandmother. She was only a teenager when the photo was taken, dressed in typical

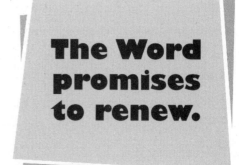

The Word promises to renew.

twenties' garb. Everyone who sees that picture thinks it is me. Now my grandmother, who is still beautiful, looks like a lot of the elderly women who live in her high-rise.

That's a revelation right there. All the external work I do profits a little. But we're all going to look pretty much the same in about forty-five years.

It's the Word that puts movement in your legs, words in your mouth, compassion in your heart, and tools in your hand. I promise you, you will no longer feel inadequate when the Word is deep inside you.

"I can't; I'm not able; I've got nothing" will soon disappear!

Chapter Eight

Why Can't My Destiny Have a Layover in Hawaii?

I 'm fat." Her voice sounded disgusted, but her face registered pure adoration.

"No, no, you're not." I will admit it was a halfhearted reply.

"Cathy, quit being nice. You *know* I'm fat," she said as she slapped her perfect size-six jeaned behind while waiting for me to say something.

We have all been in that place. She is a friend who could obviously be a top New York model, but also is filled with insecurity. Next to her, I look like a bushpig, but there I sat again, telling her how thin and beautiful she is and how the world wishes to be her.

I know it wouldn't please the Lord, but just once I would love to say, "Yes, you are really putting on weight." Instead I said, "In fact, dear, I insist you eat the last piece of pizza!" I had been hungrily eyeing it, but faster than you can say, "Hold the anchovies," she grabbed it and gobbled it up, licking her fingers.

"Oh, that was so good. I have not really eaten anything in a few days . . . that is, with the exception of the Big Mac, four Mrs. Field's cookies, and the two hot dogs, without the buns, of course . . . "

I wasn't listening to what she said because I was trying to figure out a way to nonchalantly scrape the last little bit of cheese off the lid of the pizza box without looking like a glutton.

". . . and then I finished off my son's lunch. I think it is very displeasing to the Lord to waste half a peanut butter and banana sandwich."

It was too late. Henrietta saw me, and in one swift and, what seemed to me, snotty movement, she snatched the box while clucking like a mother hen.

"No, no, no. You'll thank me later, you naughty girl. A moment on the lips, a lifetime on the hips!"

Turning away with the empty box, she took one last look at herself in the mirror. Seeming satisfied, she ran her long, manicured fingers through her gorgeous, thick mane.

We were two women, two very different women. The scene reminds me of the story in 1 Samuel about two other women who were so very different.

Hannah and Pe—Who?

It's one of my all-time favorite Bible stories. It has comforted my heart on many a long night when sleep was hard to find, but hope was present in the telling of the story. Two of our children are named after the two beloved heroes found in this book, Hannah and Samuel.

This book begins with the account of two women: one named Hannah, the other, Peninnah. Both were the wives of a man named Elkanah.

Elkanah's favorite wife was Hannah; however, as secure as she was in his love, her life was empty. She had been unable to give her husband children, and it did not help that the other wife was a fertile Myrtle.

Elkanah tried to assure Hannah that it was all right. He gave her more materially than he gave to the other wife, and he continued to pledge his love to Hannah.

Whatever! Behind his back, Peninnah provoked Hannah. It didn't matter that Hannah's living quarters were nicer, her clothes were made of better material, and she had more time on her hands to take pottery classes. She had no son.

Peninnah never let her forget it. With all of her sons and daughters, she had provided her husband with heirs, which was the most important role of the woman. It seemed as though Peninnah, not Hannah, lived in and under the blessing.

Peninnah violated all spiritual principles by using her blessing to wound and torment Hannah. Still, the very thing Hannah cried out for, Peninnah got. So unfair!

"The Prosperity of the Wicked"

Life is full of people who seem to violate the Word and get blessed. But if you allow your mind to start asking *why*, you get your head all wrapped up in the seeming inequality of God's ways, and it will destroy you. (Look at Ps. 73 if you want to think further on this matter.)

For years I would argue with God. Well, not exactly *with* God because He wasn't arguing. Here I was, a righteous woman with a righteous husband, and I desperately wanted more children, only to see some unmarried movie star having her third child with a third boyfriend.

I *so* did not want to be a Peninnah. Instead I became the party lady. I gave extravagant baby showers to every woman in our church who got pregnant. I held more than twenty-six baby showers in our home. Checking the list of baby items, I made sure each little mother got everything she needed for her miracle. I even bought and wrapped gifts and put people's names on the gift cards for those who couldn't afford to buy anything. I did it as joyfully and as lavishly as I could.

I so did not want to be a Peninnah.

But inside I was miserable.

I had gained a lot of weight, and at five-two, I tipped the scale at 265 pounds. I felt ugly, trapped, not only unloved, but unliked and abandoned. Randi and I had reached a crisis point in our marriage.

My sorrow was so great that for days I thought I would probably die, and then I was sorry that I didn't. My destiny seemed to be one of despair and defeat! The combination of sad thoughts and painful self-recrimination overwhelmed me to the point that life seemed to offer no hope at all.

During those long days, no one from our church called me. No one came to comfort me. My feelings of loneliness intensified.

After about a week, Henrietta called. She made a few stabs at polite conversation, then the well-meaning saint said, "Cathy, the Lord told me to call you." Her voice was soft as she searched for the words to comfort me, as I had done for her in the past. "Cathy, the Lord told me to never get fat like you so I'll never go through what you've been through."

It was Peninnah speaking to me. Happy wife, four children, great marriage, and a fabulous career. What would I do with this Peninnah? Would I allow her to take my dream and poison my soul?

Everything in me kept screaming out, "It's not fair. I didn't do anything wrong, yet I have to suffer. It hurts, and the pain won't go away!"

My present lay in ruins. Would I allow the enemy, who was assisted in part by a Peninnah, to rob me of my future?

Decision Time

When faced with the possible loss of my marriage, ministry, and reputation, I had to make a decision. I had to pull myself up by the maturity and the Word of God that were inside me. After hanging up the phone, I lay down on the floor and buried my face in the carpet. I prayed, much like Hannah must have prayed when she was suffering so much that she had no words. I cried, screamed, and travailed.

Somehow I let the whole world know (of course, I was alone) that God would help me. He could heal me. I was one desperate woman! Talk about "the arm of flesh will fail you, ye dare not trust your own!" Hannah had a similar problem, I believe.

I adore what Cindy Jacobs wrote in *The Women of Destiny Bible* concerning Hannah:

> Hannah was desperate. More than any other woman in the Bible. She was absolutely driven by desperation. And it drove her to a place of reckless prayer and weeping before the Lord. She abandoned her dignity, forgot formality, and begged God with all that was within her to give her a son. She had to fight for her destiny. No doubt she had to fight the consuming ache of inadequacy within her . . . and she had to fight a long and recurring battle with disappointment and, in her Old Testament culture, social disgrace.
>
> But Hannah had a fervent desire in her heart. She refused to let it go . . . She was willing to go to war in order to fulfill the destiny to which she believed God had called her. She fought with the same weapons that are available to women today—tears, prayers, faith, and passion . . . He rewarded her faith and he responded to the passion of her broken heart. (*Women of Destiny Bible* NKJV, Nelson)

Hannah was a woman of prayer. She didn't *become* a woman of prayer. Prayer was already her way of life. If *you* truly pour out your heart and soul as Hannah did, and if you truly walk with the Lord, others might think you're strange, but you'll receive a reward.

Principles of Comfort for You

These are some of the principles that God gave me during my Garden of Gethsemane. Maybe they will comfort and assist you.

- We must continue in faith. That pleases God (Col. 1:23).

- We must hold fast our hope (Heb. 3:6).

- We must continue in prayer. Remember, Hannah was praying when God answered (Rom. 12:12).

- We must continue to wait upon God. We must do what is right while we wait (Hos. 12:6).

- We must continue in well doing (2 Thess. 3:13).

I love the end of the story . . . Hannah's story *and* my story.

Hannah's story first: Eli, the priest, had two sons who were evil men and corrupt priests. God had another plan—Hannah's son, Samuel. If Hannah had given birth earlier, her son would have been too old for God's plan. If he had been born later, he would have been too young.

Everything worked together for Hannah's joy, for the people of Israel, and for the kingdom of God. God had invested the time in Hannah, preparing her so that when the day came, she could say, "Give me a son, and all the days of his life . . ." (See 1 Sam. 1:11.) She might not have been able to say that ten years earlier.

She could have given in to self-pity. In the world, people defend their right to gossip, whine, and cover jealousy with strife. Self-pity will render you

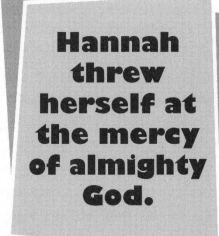

Hannah threw herself at the mercy of almighty God.

helpless and useless before God. Self-pity is a spirit. It is a part of the "self" life. *Be rid of it!*

Instead, Hannah threw herself at the mercy of almighty God. Her reward? The intangible was enormous and eternal. The tangible included three more sons and two daughters.

Do you know what happened to Peninnah's children? Me neither. The Word never names them or says they did anything worth noting.

Hannah will always be remembered, admired, and held up to emulate. On the contrary, Peninnah, God love her, is an example of a sad, hollow, temporary victory, a legacy of jealousy and bitterness.

Now my story: years later, I sat in my living room with a former pastor's wife. Her face was still beautiful, but she loathed her body and weight. Separated from her husband, she wept bitter tears as I held her, assuring her from the other side of this tragedy that, through God's grace and forgiveness, she would laugh once again. Life would be joyous, and though she might never get all the answers, healing surely would come.

That was the day I held Henrietta, my friend, in my arms. All these years later, I was able to minister to her, not out of head knowledge, but out of truth—out of personal experience and a heart that had entrusted her destiny, dreams, and well-being into the hands of a caring, loving Father.

The words spoken that day had a precious weight to them. I told her, "God will heal you. I know because He healed me. Your marriage will survive. I know because mine did. You will touch women with a hope you never knew was possible."

"Let us not grow weary while doing good, for in due season we shall reap if we do not lose heart" (Gal. 6:9).

Is there any hurt worth trading for your dream? Any offense so great to justify remaining bitter? Is there any circumstance so devastating that your heavenly Father can't be trusted to enfold you in His arms to heal and help you through your pain? Let's say it together: "Absolutely not."

You will either react like Peninnah or respond like Hannah!

Chapter Nine

Don't Settle for Half the Testimony

An incredible woman of God who is also a very dear friend shared a word about resolve. *Resolve.* It conjures up images of soldiers—hard, harsh men in camouflage with painted faces, dead eyes, a steely iron will, and total discipline. You must immediately have an image of *me*. Just kidding. I am definitely not the poster girl for resolve.

As a matter of fact, when my friend began to speak, I began to think of all the promises I have penned in the front of my Bible through the years. Written there are phrases inspired by tremendous sermons I have heard, scriptures that came alive to me during tribulations, and prophecies spoken over me that gave me a lifetime of hope. Some are dated, some are even faded, but there are probably twelve colors of ink, underlined according to how I felt at the moment. Every square inch of available space on the page is covered.

So what happened? Well, I just got a new Bible and started filling up the space in that one. I have one Bible in which I wrote down my requirements for a husband. In the back of another, there is a list of ten baby names—first, middle, and last—for every child I might have happened to bear in my lifetime. It was dated 1975, a year before I even met my beloved. Little did I realize then that my future would require faith and a resolve that I did not yet possess.

There is one thing about mountain-moving faith: you don't really have it when you start out at point A, but you will need it to get to point B. That is the purpose of this chapter. I want the Holy Spirit to awaken the promises and prophecies that perhaps you have written in the back of *your* Bible but never learned how to acquire. Could it be that life zapped your energy to fight for your great destiny, and now it hurts just to think about those promises? You might feel like Delta Dawn, the aging bride from the song of the same name, who is still waiting at the bus stop for her true love to come back to her. What is so sad is that she is still in her wedding dress.

It's Never Too Late to Begin Again

At this moment, as I sit here in my dining room, typing away on my 1907 Swingtec typewriter, my three-year-old is at my elbow doing exactly what three-year-olds do when their mothers are not putting them at the center of the universe. In the last hour, she has managed to get a video stuck in the DVD player, trim one ear of our miniature poodle, dump half a box of Froot Loops on the floor (I'm thinking that was not an accident), and throw herself down, crying because I won't let her play with my typewriter. The poodle has now thrown up, probably due to the trauma of seeing his new asymmetrical haircut, compliments of my now screaming toddler.

The incredible part about this is that everything from my cluttered, elegant dining room to my three-year-old daughter can be traced back to a hastily scribbled promise written in the back of my Bible. My home was nothing more than a desire so far out of my reach that anyone with any sense begged me to give it up. Anytime you have a dream, you risk being disappointed. But many Christians *won't* risk their hearts because it hurts too much if the promise doesn't come immediately. That may be safer, but it takes all the joy out of life. Of course, there is risk involved, but isn't that what a life full of faith is all about?

> There is risk involved, but isn't that what a life full of faith is all about?

I believe that by the time you finish reading this chapter, that little, itty-bitty, teensy, tiny speck of seed that would not die will start jumping up and down inside you, saying, "Hey, I'm still in here. My name is Destiny, and if you will just allow yourself to hope again, God will bring your promise to pass." (If that little seed begins saying anything more, such as, "Leave your rotten husband, Mildred, and move to Tulsa and marry Carman," then you need to back up a little and make sure what you hear is at least biblical.)

Delay Is Not Necessarily Denial

My precious, what is the incredible dream that God has invested in your heart? Is it not worth standing and fighting for? Do you know anyone who just became tired of standing and finally gave up, only to live a life wondering why God was not answering his or her prayers? Have *you* questioned why it seems that others are being blessed, with the heavens open to them, while you are not?

I know a wonderful Christian guy who has a call to ministry in his life. He is probably the most miserable man on the planet a majority of the time. He just cannot seem to figure out why life is so unfair. We have talked for hours while I gently (at least I think I am being gentle) shared the simple principles that the Word of God teaches us as Christians to incorporate into our lives. I call these the kingdom principles—basic concepts that will cause the favor and blessing of God to rest on us.

Years ago, when this man was a young intern in the ministry, a senior pastor treated him very badly. He was overworked and underpaid. The pastor never gave him any honor. Because of the insecurities my friend carried around in his mind, the enemy badgered him with accusations against the pastor and the church elders and basically wore him out emotionally. As a young man, he walked around the church like a keg of explosives ready to go off at any time to anyone. The bitterness of his soul finally led to his being fired.

This man has an undisputed tremendous ministry gifting, so in spite of his termination, he began a string of great ministry positions. As it says in Proverbs 18:16, "A man's gift makes room for him."

But it wasn't long before the grievance that had been carried over from each church would come up again. All the old feelings of inequality, injustice, resentment, and anger would resurface. As a young man, my friend had a reputation with the district of his denomination as a troublemaker and a rebel. Every time we talked, I had to hear the story of the latest unfair pastor. Finally in a fit of despair, he decided he was not even called to the ministry. Without giving any notice, he walked out.

He felt that everyone was out to get him and that even God had turned His back on him. Selling his birthright and inheritance, he went into the business world. I thought that when he married, perhaps his wife, a shy Christian girl, might encourage and help him return to his call. But her own fears and insecurities kept them out of the ministry, and they eventually attended church only sporadically. The enemy won.

The couple now has four lovely daughters who for years have listened to their parents' hurts and hostilities every Sunday from the backseat of their minivan on the way home from their latest church. Those little girls are now angry young women who want nothing to do with the church or with Christians in general. They are causing their parents deep heartache.

In our last conversation, my once angry young friend, now an angrier middle-aged man, wept while saying, "What happened to my daughter Susie? I simply don't know what to do with her. She is so angry and so depressed."

I wanted to yell out over the phone, "You blockhead! [Now, isn't that just lovely?] What did you think was going to happen? You are looking in the mirror at an image of yourself! The way you feel is only a small part of what God has felt about what you have done with your life and ministry."

But I said nothing like that. I listened and said all the appropriate ahs and ums. I added, "I'm so sorry." What a heartbreak! What a waste! But—and this a very big *but*—I believe that my dear friend will one day get sick and tired of being sick and tired and cry out to his Savior. God in His infinite mercy and patience, who has waited for me so many times that it is embarrassing, will deliver, minister to, and heal my friend.

God loves us enough to wait us out. He also loves us enough not to give in to us while we have ourselves a forty-year tantrum. He just waits. Since we have been created in His image, it occurred to me that God was trying to develop that same godly character in me. It's *the ability to wait.*

God loves us enough to wait us out.

Do not, and I repeat, *do not* close this book. These next few pages are rather like an exercise. It may be really hard, but you know it's good for you. It may be really, really hard, but it's really, really good for you. You get the idea?

Am I Supposed to Lay It on the Altar or Stand in Faith Without Wavering?

The answer to that question is . . . yes. How many times I believed that this was the month I was pregnant, only to weep in disappointment and despair when I discovered I wasn't. It would have been easier to deal with the *why* questions and do what my friend did. I could have gotten angry with God. I could have felt hurt, resentful, and bitter because God wasn't keeping His promise. Instead, I sneaked off to the bathroom and cried.

I'm not saying I didn't struggle with those thoughts. There was the temptation to sit down and have a great big pity party for myself. My friend, if you truly desire to see your dream and destiny fulfilled, self-pity is *not* the way to go.

The greatest lesson I learned from my sixteen-year battle with infertility (and you are supposed to learn lessons) was to keep my heart from bitterness at all costs. Esau lost his birthright over it. David's wife, Michal, was stricken with barrenness. David's brother Eliab lost a place in David's kingdom. Judas resented the money coming into the treasury and lost his life over his foible. All those men and women once had an opportunity for greatness until they allowed bitterness to poison their souls.

Serve the Promiser, Not the Promise

If there is ever a misstep that we take when seeking our future in God's kingdom, it is that we live for the promise, not for the Promiser.

I have witnessed lives that fell apart when there was a delay or when God needed to alter the plan. Is that what God expects of me? No, when my dreams are detained, in my attitude toward the Father, I take those dreams, those visions, and those desires, and lay them at His feet. He alone has the ability to bring them to pass. I must trust that He has it all under control.

I am not living at the whim of an angry God who dangles a future and a hope in front of me just as one would dangle a carrot in front of a donkey and then yank it away. He doesn't throw back His head and laugh because I am heaven's after-dinner amusement. That is *not* the heart of the God I love and serve.

He will work a heart in you that will cry out:

My Father, I love You. You have done incredible things for me, and I am eternally grateful. My heart is heavy for the fulfillment of the undone promises. I do not know why this desire has not come to pass. I am tempted to get discouraged, my Lord, and I do not want to. I refuse to blame You. I refuse to indulge in self-pity or the sin of the children of Israel.

So with all I have and all that is within me, I will to worship You, trusting that You are my Father, my Friend, and my King, and You will fulfill Your word to me. And if You know that I am standing and believing for the wrong destiny, or at the wrong time, please adjust me, Lord. I live for You. I do not live for what You can do.

> **Prayer is the key to seeing the reality of promises come to pass.**

Dear friend, if you will read that prayer again out loud, liberty and hope and comfort will begin to drive out the feelings of weariness and loneliness. The attack of the enemy is to lie about the character of our God so that you will begin to distrust Him. But trust is the key element of our faith.

Faith is the key element of mountain-moving prayer. Prayer is the key to seeing the reality of promises come to pass before we are too ancient to enjoy them.

If the enemy cannot get you to doubt and become frustrated with God, he then tries another tactic. He will stir a few of your "friends" to challenge the voice of God. He may even use your own family.

Joseph, the dreamer, learned a heartbreaking lesson when he shared his dreams with his half brothers. They mocked him and scorned him for having the pride and audacity to infer that he would be promoted to a place of honor that would cause even their parents to bow down to him.

The lesson? Never share your dreams with half brothers because not everyone will celebrate your dream.

Are We There Yet? Are We There Yet? Are We There Yet? Are We . . .

Unless you are a multigazillionaire, chances are that you have had to personally drive your children to school, to dance class, to soccer games, to church, to doctors' visits, and to Disney World. (I have an incredible notion about how to drive any terrorists out of their feeble minds: let them take my children by car to somewhere that is more than thirty-five minutes away.) And during all that driving, how many times have you heard, "Are we there yet?"

The Lord expects us to use all the available tools that have been given to us that are perfect to assist us in bringing in our promises. I have spoken at numerous meetings around the world. When people realize that God uses me in prophecy, they really put their faith out there for me to minister to them and give them a "word." Usually they already have four or five "words" from God, a couple of Technicolor visions, and sixteen confirmations. Still, they want "just one more" to confirm that God does really hear and answer prayer.

In God's ears, it must sound like "Are we there yet?" repeated again and again. What is the actual answer to that question? My father answered us with exasperation and said, "We will be there when we get there. Now stop asking me anymore." Of course, that didn't stop us from asking him a hundred more times until we finally got there.

Make Your Journey a Joyful One

Your journey can be a joy, or it can be a miserable ride with a detour right back to the beginning. Your choice. The question you need to answer is, *How do I get there?* The answer? Resolve.

Resolve? It means to answer, to explain, to fix, and to make work again. It also means to make up one's mind. Resolve means that you actually navigate from point A to point B. Without true resolve, you may never see your promises come to pass. Some think that their promises will just fall from the sky, never realizing that God desires for them to be active participants in bringing their dreams to pass.

But resolve has *you* finishing the story! So resolve to determine that no ending to your testimony is acceptable except the one that God has told you is out there for you. Become a woman of strong resolve, and no one can rob you of your exciting journey!

Chapter Ten

Lord, Is That Your Voice I Heard or Just the Pizza I Ate Last Night?

Refusing to allow my face to betray what was happening in my heart at that moment required all the training of an Academy Award–winning actress.

Continuing to smile, all the while batting my eyes rapidly so as not to let one tear escape, I nodded my head as the love of my life explained that he just wasn't ready to walk down the aisle. The load of his ministry, he explained, was so heavy. The invitations to preach were pouring in, and the Lord was asking him to lay down his fiancée—me—to be devoted to his call for a season.

My cheeks were flaming hot while my body began to shiver. Rejection. Gallantly taking me into his arms, he told me nothing had really changed. He still loved me, and we would marry . . . just a little later.

Making a pretense of looking at his watch, a dead giveaway

because he looked at the wrong wrist, he was completely surprised at the lateness of the hour . . . according to his wrist hair.

He promised to call that night as soon as he got settled in to the church where he was starting a new revival. Of course, if the service was long and he had to go out to dinner with the pastor and his wife, he would wait and call tomorrow. He didn't want to take the chance of waking me up.

And with those words, he was gone. The last I saw of him were the brake lights on his '65 Chevy Impala.

He did not call that night. I consoled myself with the thought that because he was such a wonderful man of God, he would honor his word to the pastor and his wife.

The next day, I stayed home from work because I wouldn't want my true love to call and not find me there. I took the phone and put it on my pillow. I went to the bathroom and left the door open so I could run and grab the phone. After all, if it rang more than three or four times, he might think I wasn't home.

By the end of the week I was frantic. He must be in a hospital somewhere because of an accident that occurred while driving to his next meeting. He was probably so distraught over the pain he had caused me that, blinded by tears, he swerved into oncoming traffic and was hit by a concrete truck. Now he lay in the hospital in a coma. I hoped he had on clean underwear.

Never in my life had I been so forward as to call a man. My Southern upbringing actually forbade it. Women who called men were deemed loose, desperate, and low class. I spent my entire Saturday calling, leaving messages, and trying not to sound like what I was becoming. No one seemed to know where Slade was. (I just made that name up, but wouldn't it be cool to have a fiancé named Slade Roan Rittenhouserworth III? The story, however, is sadly true.)

It was another three months before I heard from my future groom. Three months of anguish, self-recrimination, and rejection. I went over every detail of our last conversation, searching for some hint of what I could have said. It actually never occurred to me that *I* was not the problem. The enemy had me so oppressed that I did not realize how warped my thinking had become over the issue.

A Cruel Weapon

Welcome to the spirit of rejection. It has to be one of the cruelest weapons in Satan's arsenal. If all I accomplish with this book is to see precious, gorgeous people of God delivered from the spirit of rejection and healed from the ravages of its power, then I will consider this endeavor a huge success.

The next time I heard from my fiancé was through the mail. The envelope sat on the dining room table. It was a large, fat envelope with fancy script writing, addressed to Miss Cathy Lee Rothert, my maiden name. Why would he send me a formally addressed letter? Finally taking the envelope to my bedroom and sitting on the bed, I turned it over carefully, sliding a fingernail under the seal of the precious missive.

What I saw made my entire world come crumbling down. Reading the words several times over did not help. I read them again. Perhaps the tenth time I read them, a part of my brain—you know, the center part that you never, ever use, the part reserved only for Greek tragedy—began to throb. (If I had looked in the mirror at that point,

I'm sure I would have seen my forehead pulsing in and out like a Klingon from *Star Trek*.)

Dr. and Mrs. Quantum L. Birdsnot

and

Po and LaLa Rittenhouserworth II

request your presence at the marriage of their children,

Princess Buttercup

and

the man you wouldn't marry if he were the last living soul on the

face of the earth,

Slade "PePe" Rittenhouserworth III

Reception immediately following in

the West Wing of the White House

The happy couple will depart for a month-long honeymoon in Bali because the bride's family is stinking rich and she will never have to believe God for anything in her entire life.

I sat on the edge of my bed in Jupiter, Florida, and sobbed (I did not make that up). I was a nineteen-year-old pastor's daughter with a minimum-wage-paying job that I hated and a Sunday school class that I loved, and I thought my life was over.

I had been thrown away, and no matter how much I cried and how much I prayed, I could not make the pain go away. Counting backward, I soon figured out that he had been engaged to both of us at the same time. What I couldn't reconcile was the *why*. Why did he choose her instead of me? Why would any human being ever treat someone that way? What did I do to make him change his mind?

On and on the questions came. It was the first thing on my mind in the morning and the last thing I thought about before crying myself to sleep at night.

My precious mother sat with me at night trying to convince me that if he was that sort of man, he didn't deserve me to begin with. Mom finally boxed up the wedding dress and took it back to Bridal Gowns by the Hour. She canceled the invitations and talked the pots and pans salesman into tearing up the contract by letting him come back and get his 2-, 4-, 5-, 6-, and 12-quart saucepans with matching lids, along with the free turkey baster.

But there was something she did not return. I did not find out about it until later. She carefully wrapped the bridal veil in layers of tissue, treating it as though it was something holy rather than an object of derision and embarrassment.

Six months later, she retrieved it from the top of her closet. It was the same shelf where she always hid our Christmas presents and thought we didn't know. We had both fallen in love with the veil the minute we saw it. It was my childhood dream—a Juliet cap covered in tiny pearls, from which flowed a full-length veil.

When you are nineteen and something happens that breaks your heart, you make all sorts of silly vows, vows that are just waiting to be broken. Mom kept that veil, not only because I loved it, but also because it represented a hope that I would love again.

Forgiving from the Heart

Life can be cruel at times, but the neat part about it all is that you don't die. You can live your life by biblical principles, even if other people don't (and even if it seems that those who do wrong are blessed, and that part of your brain is going to have a meltdown).

I have absolutely no idea what happened to Slade and Princess Buttercup. I never heard from either of them again. Maybe they were upset because I couldn't make the wedding. I guess I should have gotten them a Tupperware lettuce spinner—I love mine. I always doubted that Princess B. could actually burp a bowl.

I do know, however, what happened to me. God's command to forgive is not really optional. He doesn't *suggest* that we forgive. He *commands* that we forgive. God's Word even expects that we forgive *from the heart* (Matt. 18:35). That means that the hurt inflicted by the person who broke my heart, though I may remember it, is now *as though it never happened*. If I have forgiven properly, the pain associated with the event is gone, fading away into a hazy memory.

> ## God's Word even expects that we forgive from the heart.

People in ministry often say that "you forgive, and true forgiveness forgets." But God doesn't suck out your brain and your memories with a steam vac. I well remember some of the unkind words that have been spoken. Yet God said the only answer acceptable to Him is forgiveness.

Unforgiveness can bring much emotional torment. Giving the enemy a toehold will bring you physical torment. Besides, what I sow is the very thing I will reap. If I sow forgiveness and mercy, then I receive forgiveness and mercy. It does not matter whether the wrongdoer wounded me intentionally or not. True forgiveness means that I cannot continue to hold on to my grief even if the offense was biblically wrong. *I* reap what *I* sow. I don't have to reap what *you* sow. Hallelujah! How liberating!

It did not happen overnight. It did not happen in a month. In fact, I really don't know when it happened. There was just a day, after many long days of continually forgiving, that I did not hurt anymore.

Only God can do that; however, we have to do our part. It is an exercise of our wills in the middle of the temptation to have a pity party. I can be the queen of pity parties. If it was possible, some of *you* could probably make the devil feel sorry for you! But the only thing you and I get by insisting on throwing a fit will be the alienation of the people who really love us. All of us have a great dislike for being around people who throw temper tantrums (though, if we were really honest, we would admit we have really thrown some doozies). We need to realize that only by doing it God's perfect way will we receive the blessing.

So What Did God Say?

One of my favorite passages of Scripture was made so real to me after this broken engagement. I have used it many times over the years.

> Therefore, behold, I will allure her,
> Will bring her into the wilderness,
> And speak comfort to her.
> I will give her her vineyards from there,
> And the Valley of Achor as a door of hope;

> She shall sing there,
>
> As in the days of her youth,
>
> As in the day when she came up from the land of Egypt.
>
> "And it shall be, in that day,"
>
> Says the LORD,
>
> "That you will call Me 'My Husband,'
>
> And no longer call Me 'My Master.'" (Hos. 2:14–16)

The Lord gives us a little peek into the mode of operations. The word *allure* gives me a picture of near seduction, a carrot dangled in front of the donkey. Except that the One holding the carrot, the Master, is not there to tease the donkey. He is there to save the donkey's life. God says, "Darling, what you need is not going to be found anywhere except in the place I am going to take you."

Yes, Lord, let's go!

Yipes! Yes, Lord, let's go! Then you wake up and see that you are in the middle of a wilderness. Worse, most of your friends are in their own wildernesses and are not interested in talking about *your* latest trial. They want to talk about theirs. That is when you cry out; that is when you are tempted to believe that it is your husband's fault, your pastor's fault, or even the devil's fault.

It is no one's fault. It is the divine path, those ordered steps we love to talk about where God is leading us, and we will either follow or die in the wilderness trying to lead ourselves out.

Then something totally incredible happens. We hear God's voice clearly, more clearly than we have ever heard Him speak before. All the distractions of the city are gone in the wilderness. He begins to comfort us, holding us and kissing us like a mother tenderly kisses the boo-boos of her child. The valley sprouts up with a vineyard.

In the natural world, that could never happen. There is no water, and the sand won't grow anything. The seed would die long before it had a chance to take root. But we are not natural women, are we? It is amazing to me how God can turn those horrible, barren places into fruitful ground. Out of the fruit from the vineyard in your wilderness you can feed others. New wine and fresh veggies, bread right from the spiritual oven, and meat that has not turned rancid.

> **He begins to comfort us, holding us and kissing us like a mother.**

People, especially hurting people, know when what they are being given in their valley is fresh or not. I cringe inside when I happen to be going through a challenge and some well-meaning Christian tries to minister to me out of his or her lack. Have you ever tried to eat a tree branch or a cup of sand and dirt? It is distasteful in your mouth, and you want to spit it out.

But when you have the goods, others will line up at your front door for a little glass of water or a sip of wine, something that will strengthen them for another day of battle.

Trouble Becoming Hope

If I am going to have to go through the wilderness anyway, let me have something to show for it. Let me share the anointing that came on me when I was in the midnight hour of my life and I cried out to God to either change me or take me home.

Something else incredible happens. Verse 15 says, "I will give her . . . the Valley of Achor as a door of hope." The word *Achor*, literally translated, means "trouble." How amazing is that? So let's read that again with this new meaning. "I will give her . . . the Valley of Trouble [and it will become] her hope."

What you see as a terrible mess, a grievous situation, God sees entirely differently. He says that weakness will now become a doorway for your miracle. Just a minute! I think I am going to have a little shout!

Okay, I did. That ministers to me so much even as I'm sitting here in my dining room in Jacksonville, Florida, writing this. I pray that the Holy Spirit will communicate it to you as well. The very next part of the verse declares, "She shall sing there . . . as in the day when she came up from the land of Egypt."

The day we came out of Egypt was a very good day. Do you remember what Miriam sang after the Israelites crossed over the Red Sea? She led a tambourine special of "Sing to the Lord, for He has triumphed gloriously! The horse and its rider He has thrown into the sea!" (Ex. 15.21). If you are not singing, you are not coming up out of the wilderness. It is as simple as that. No singing, no leaving, period. That should get some of you off the couch and moving—no, running—toward your destiny.

In the very next verse God actually draws us into an intimacy, a relationship that goes from my Master to my Husband.

A boss has certain rights over you. It's business. You work, you go home, and you get paid.

A husband is very different. He loves you and takes care of you. Everything that he owns is also yours by law. You have the public relationship, but you also have the bedroom relationship. You know each other intimately, and that is what God says He gives to those who follow Him into the wilderness without complaining. That is what He gives to those who persevere when all they see in the natural is sand. They keep going until the harvest, which is God's investment in them, comes forth.

You begin to sing because all your tears of sorrow are gone, and you just do not feel like fighting anymore. Sing, sweetheart, sing! Why? Because the Lord of the harvest is your Fiancé. He will never leave you at the altar for another. He cannot lie. He lives just to hear your voice and delights when you come away by your own choice.

Emerging from the Hurt

So whatever happened to my broken heart? After several really difficult months, the Spirit of God brought me out of the hurt. I said the words *I forgive you* numerous times to the picture I kept secretly hidden at my bedside. I suppose other people would think I was crazy, but I know that the principle of "whatsoever he saith" (Mark 11:23) has power in it. I also had to drag my spirit man into the Holy of Holies every single day and tell myself that I *would* praise. God honored my feeble attempts. Really, that is all He desires for us to do: just grab our rebellious flesh and worship Him. He does the rest.

Three short years later, during one of the happiest times of my single life, I was invited to a church service to hear a Jewish missionary preach in a Foursquare church. That was on Friday. I was asked to sing a solo that night, and the incredibly good-looking evangelist asked me if I would like to go out for a cup of coffee after the service.

My experiences with good-looking guest speakers had not exactly been a success. I still, to this day, do not know why I went for coffee with this one. But six weeks later, I went to the altar with the man who would become my best friend, my lover, and the holder of all my dreams.

I got to wear my wedding dress and my beautiful veil with the Juliet cap. A couple of weeks ago I even dragged the wedding dress and veil from the attic and watched while my five daughters took turns wearing it and having their pictures taken. (Give me a break! There was a hurricane warning, and we were all bored!)

It won't be long until the day comes for me to hold on to my daughters' dreams. Until then, though, I am going to sit here and type with my veil on my head.

Chapter Eleven

Out of Medication with Half of Life to Go

What was the smell? I couldn't seem to place it. While I tried to adjust my eyes to the light in the room, the flickering images of the television caught my attention.

I must have fallen asleep with the TV on. Before me was a man demonstrating the use of an aerosol spray can of Instant Hair. It was so awful that I continued to watch. You know, like passing a dead cat on the side of the road. You know it will be grotesque, but you can't look away.

Speaking of dead cats, by the time the guy had covered half of his head in brown spray paint, he appeared to have something dead on the top. The studio audience clapped with joy at the transformation, and the man with the painted head assured us that now he had the confidence he needed to get that better job or go after the tons of beautiful women who would surely want him.

The jangle of the telephone made me jump, and the reverie was broken. "Good morning, Mrs. Lechner, this is your wake-up call."

"Yes, thank you, and exactly what time is it?"

"It's 6:00 A.M., and the temperature here is thirty-one degrees with snow flurries."

Great, I thought. "And just exactly where is 'here'?"

"I beg your pardon, Mrs. Lechner?"

Again I asked, "Where am I?"

Thinking I was drunk, the woman on the other end of the phone switched from her polite wake-up-call voice to her you-are-wasting-my-time-and-I-am-embarrassed-for-you voice: "You are in Needlebrow, Minnesota."

Needlebrow, Needlebrow . . . nope, that didn't ring a bell.

"Ma'am, is there a larger city that we might be near?"

Her patience was gone. What kind of an idiot doesn't know where she is? I can answer that. The kind that spends fifty weekends a year traveling; that's the kind.

"We are in between Scurvy City and Cheese Hole, and if you flew in, you came into Benidine International."

"There is an international airport in Benidine?"

"Well, they fly into Canada and that is a foreign country." The lady at the switchboard was dripping with sarcasm at the fact that I, a world traveler, was apparently not aware that Canada was another country.

Thanking her, I hung up the phone, swung my legs away from the bed, and reluctantly planted my feet on the mildewy carpet. (I'd finally identified the lovely smell.)

Pain! That was all my brain could register. Terrible pain, starting in the lower back and continuing down my leg into my left foot.

Now I remember! I went to bed in agony last night. I had stood for three hours the previous morning and another four hours that evening teaching the Word and personally ministering to several hundred people afterward. All the standing, plus the long plane ride the day before, had triggered an attack of sciatica so severe it left me in writhing pain.

I had to preach in two more services on Sunday morning, and I could not even stand up. How was I ever going to get my clothes on, much less stand and preach?

Zapped!

Pain is a huge roadblock to being able to pursue our destiny. It has the power to zap our strength, steal our joy, and rob our energy. Yet we are warned that the testing of our faith works patience. Pain, whether it is physical or emotional, eats away at our enthusiasm and our sense of hope until just getting through the day is sometimes all that we can do.

I have been blessed with an incredibly kind and compassionate Christian doctor who has been helping me walk through this nightmare called a herniated disc. Years ago, when someone told me he had a back problem, I would give him that "Oh, brother, what a wimp" look and tell him to suck it up and keep going. I do not do that anymore.

Swallowing two pain pills I grabbed from the nightstand, I lay back on the pillow, waiting for relief. It was taking longer and longer to bring the pain into any manageable condition, and this morning was no exception. Time was running out, and I was left with just enough of it to shower, dress, and apply makeup to my pasty face.

When people find out that a fellow believer has any kind of an aliment, they are moved with compassion to lay hands on you and pray for your healing. That is the very reason I do not tell anyone when I am in pain.

Once a prayer warrior assembled the other prayer warrior sisters to pray for me. It would have been very moving if it had not been downright comical. Ten pairs of hands accompanied by ten serious, driven intercessors were shaking me and praying so loud that I would also need to have my hearing healed.

Every five minutes or so, the chief warrior would silence the others to ask if I was healed yet. I was thinking that a simple, but truthful "no" would allow them to graciously say the right Christian phrases with hugs all around and then we could all go home.

"Come, ladies, this is a stubborn spirit. Let's intensify." The hands suddenly weighed what seemed like fifty more pounds, and the prayers became more deafening.

I thought, *Please, God, just give me a little something for these ladies. They are so earnest.*

It took three tries and me telling them "no" each time . . . but maybe I felt a little twinge in my back. I prayed there would be because I did not think I could stand much more prayer.

Enough Blame to Go Around

Transparency, a subject I touched on a few chapters ago, can be an incredible blessing to those who hear your story and receive hope. The flip side of being so transparent with your life is that you also open yourself up for judgments. That happened to me on a couple of occasions.

A pastor's wife pulled me to the side to tell me that if I had not yet been healed, there was a problem. She felt as though God showed her that I had a secret sin. I asked her if she would now ask God what it was, because it was so secret that even I didn't know what it was. Fully understanding the principle that sin can hinder your healing, I certainly did not take lightly what she desired to share with me. But I had searched my heart and opened up to my pastor and husband for correction and even rebuke.

No one wants to walk around the same old stupid mountain for the rest of one's life. This pastor's wife suggested not so subtly that perhaps I had some immorality going on in my life. I didn't mean to laugh, but the words popped out of my mouth before I could stop them.

No one wants to walk around the same old stupid mountain for the rest of one's life.

"Do you know how many children I have? Seven! I am in church every weekend. My free time is used up writing books, preparing sermons, and cooking dinners for eleven. When exactly would I have time for moral failure? I am never alone. Usually a member of my staff, my husband, or a child is with me 24/7. I barely have enough energy for my own husband, much less some else's."

She immediately retracted her pointy finger, murmured something about being sorry, and then left.

We are so quick to assign blame. We blame either God or the devil. Well, I think it's because you fell and twisted your back and herniated two discs. Now you are doing everything within your power to stand on the Word of God and His promises to heal you. The devil comes in, in his attempts to keep you down. You feel so overwhelmed that you do not want to fight anymore. You don't even want to get out of bed some mornings.

A well-meaning pastor told me flat out that I was not healed because my faith was not great enough. I asked him what more I could do to increase my faith. All I need is a tiny grain of a mustard seed of it to move an entire mountain. I really believed that I had that much.

God had asked me to follow Him. When my body ached so badly that I could hardly breathe without pain, I still followed Him. The minute I stood up to minister the Word of God, the anointing of the Holy Spirit came upon me, and the pain was gone. I was aware only of His presence and His power and His desire to touch people through me.

Giving Up Is *Not* the Answer

Listen, my dear friend. The enemy of your soul delights in sabotaging your destiny. If he cannot get you to fill your heart with bitterness and unforgiveness, he will tempt you to give up. Many give up, and that is so sad. You don't have to give up. You can get through your pain and possess the promise that God has for you.

"But, Cathy, how do I ignore my pain? It takes every bit of my attention."

I know. I really know.

I would like to share a few small principles that I have learned going through life that may encourage you.

A Remarkable Story

There is an old story of how Queen Victoria held a banquet for her soldiers who had won the Victoria Cross Medal of Bravery. It was a special feast, a royal banquet with all the glittering pomp of a royal palace. The guests came from every walk of life, which included the rich and the poor. Their only qualification for being there was outstanding bravery.

Among the guests was a very poor, uneducated soldier, completely bewildered by such an array of regal splendor. The table sparkled with gleaming cutlery such as his eyes had never seen before. Trembling, he picked up a finger bowl and drank from it. There was a titter of laughter accompanied by subdued snickers and superior smiles from those around him.

You can get through your pain and possess the promise that God has for you.

As he blushed with embarrassment, the queen saw what had happened. She leaned forward, picked up a finger bowl, her eyes flashing fire, and drank from it. Then with a resounding thump she placed it on the table. And as the queen slowly looked around the royal table with her eyes still flashing, the smirks and snickers died and heads bowed. She, the great queen of the British Empire, had identified herself with her humble soldier.

That is what my Jesus did: "And the Word was made flesh" (John 1:14 KJV). It comforts me to know not only that He understands my pain, but also that He suffered pain. When the cry goes out from a drowning man, his would-be rescuer kicks off his shoes, throws aside his coat, and dives into the very conditions he seeks to save the struggling victim from. *He must overcome to undertake!* He is of no service if he sinks.

The years Jesus was on the earth became proof that He was fit to be the Savior of mankind. Spotless and sinless in heaven as the divine Son of God, He kicked off the shoes of untried, untempted Divinity, threw aside His royal robe, and plunged into our fallen world as a man.

It is one thing for a man who is on the roof to issue instructions to a man in the garden on how to climb the wall. It is another thing for the man on the roof to come down and get under him and lift him up.

Jesus Learned Not to Live . . . but to Let Another Live Through Him

Jesus learned obedience through and by the way He suffered. His suffering was in His yielding. He destroyed the impetuous compulsion.

When you speak of the pressures of life, you are unconsciously declaring your resistance. I am called on to suffer every now and then, and just as Jesus learned obedience, so must I. I do not live in misery like the old saints did years ago, thinking that was somehow pleasing to God.

There were those in my father's church who would be first to stand up on testimony night. I especially remember, even though I was a child, a particular elderly woman who would raise her hand to indicate she had a testimony. You could hear a collective sigh throughout the congregation. Even at my young age, I knew it wasn't going to edify anyone.

She started out with her head bowed down and one hand raised to heaven. Then for a full ten minutes she would talk about her dead relatives, her mean-as-a-hound-dog husband, and the fact that even though she had no money, no food, and they were going to turn off the electricity for nonpayment, she still thanked the Lord.

My brother Harold could do a great imitation of her. Don't get upset; it's just preacher's kids stuff. When your whole social life is spent in the church, you need entertainment. Sister Beasley was

> **God's Son learned to say "Amen" to God.**

ours. If you were not a Christian, Sister Beasley made you never want to become one. If you were a Christian, Sister Beasley made you want to look into Hare Krishna. She had a life full of suffering, but to what purpose?

Jesus' suffering had purpose. His suffering taught Him obedience. God's Son learned to say "Amen" to God, who permitted in His wisdom what He could have prevented in His power.

Men who dedicate themselves to warfare must submit themselves to the discipline of a drilled army. The issue is life or death. There is no "please, gentlemen, may I have your attention." It's "atten-shun, quick, march left, right, left, right . . ." I am not even permitted to walk at my own pace. Obedience is never obedience unless it is instant. This is the lesson of obedience.

One dear woman of God, whom I respect highly not only for her teaching gift, but also for her life spent with the One she simply calls "my Teacher," suffers from debilitating physical problems.

The first time I saw her was when her husband was wheeling her up to the platform in a wheelchair. She was bent over, and I remember thinking, *Who is that woman, and why are they letting her get up on the platform with the speakers?*

This five-foot little lady rose from her chair, and I could see she was stooped over. When she got to the pulpit, something amazing happened. I saw the Holy Spirit come upon her as she rose up straight and began to teach the Word with the most awesome revelation and anointing I have ever been privileged to witness. When she talked about her Teacher, she made it sound as though He was a lover, as though it was a relationship with a man that had such intimacy that it made you weep as she shared.

Truthfully I was jealous of her relationship with Him. She talked about Him in such a way that even though I love and serve Him, I simply had to acknowledge that I didn't have what she did. I found out later, after spending much time talking with this beautiful and regal woman of God, what a price she paid to have this incredible relationship, this love affair that made her face glow with His glory when she said His name.

She told me how, during a ministry trip abroad, a woman hugged her with such enthusiasm that it broke several vertebrae and released osteoporosis that led to severe arthritis and disabled her.

Because of her poor physical condition, no one would dare have blamed her for staying home. Yet she continued to travel all over the world. She was not a young woman who could deal with her infirmities knowing she had a lifetime. She was an elderly woman who could have told everyone, "I don't feel good, and I'm not coming to minister."

I asked her *why* once, why all the hassles of air travel and hotel beds and often feeling underappreciated for all her sacrifice?

She smiled at me as she put her lovely manicured hand with skin so transparent I could see the veins of her hand and said, "Daughter, because my Teacher asked me to." She then went back to eating her soup. Everything was an effort, but she lives to hear His, "Well done, My child."

Many are the times I have hung my head in shame because as bad as she felt, I never once heard her complain. I pretty much complain to anyone who will listen. I saw in me a secret spirit of pride shut up in my heart that wanted people to know how hard traveling was and wanted to make them feel sorry for me.

Yes, Serious Seekers Confront Sorrow Too

You, my friend, if you are serious about possessing the destiny God has for you, will be asked to drink from the cup of sorrow at some point in your life.

I remember the day when a lady walked up to my elderly friend just as she was being seated in her wheelchair after delivering an awesome two-and-a-half-hour sermon. The woman took my friend's hand and said she wanted to pray for her; she said she perceived that my friend had a spirit of unforgiveness and resentment that blocked her from God's healing. I took a couple of steps backward.

I saw a look come into my friend's eyes that I have never seen before in anyone. She drew herself up out of that chair to her full height, which seemed to me to be ten feet tall. Pointing her finger in the woman's face, she said, "God did not do this to me." And then she whispered the rest, which unfortunately I did not hear. I bet it was something absolutely great. The poor lady just sort of shriveled, mumbled her apology, and left.

I thought at the time, *Why would anyone presume upon such a woman who has demonstrated the depth and width of God's love?* It would be like standing at the foot of Calvary and telling Jesus, "I know why You are up there. You must have secret sin."

Decision for Your Destiny

So there are two things, at least, to remember when you're faced with the critical decision of moving forward into your wilderness or returning to Egypt.

1. Do not throw rocks at other people who are on the same road as you.

2. Do not yell at people in wheelchairs.

No, these are not really the exact two things, even though they may help. *These* are the ones to remember:

1. Don't despise your suffering, but grab hold of the maturity in the Word that is inside you. That pleases God.

2. Trials are temporary and everybody has them, so rejoice!

Chapter Twelve

May the Glory Electrify You

The woman who stood in front of me was clearly not the same woman who had stood in the exact same place one year earlier. With big tears rolling down her face, she used the back of her hand to wipe her runny nose. I followed that hand in case it might try to find its way to me. I know . . . I'm a wimp. It was then that I heard the Holy Spirit say, *Cathy, hold this woman. Put your arms around her as you would one of your little children, and speak tenderly to her.*

The moment I put my arms around her and pulled her to me, all the resistance in her melted away. She lay in my arms, weeping. As I kissed her hair, touched her face, and used my hand to wipe away the bitter tears, all the hurt and anger that had been bottled up for so long came pouring out.

It's funny the things that you remember when such incidents

happen. What stands out in my mind was that I had on a new white linen dress. I had been waiting to wear that dress for a long time. It had been ten pounds too small when I bought it, but now it fit. I had found matching shoes and a shoulder bag. I was smokin'! (That's teenager talk for "I really looked good!")

By the time I finished praying for this precious woman, a half hour had passed. Stopping by the bathroom on the way out of the church, I looked in the mirror. To my horror, I saw that the shoulder of my new dress was covered in beige foundation, black mascara, and red lipstick. Grabbing for the paper towel roll was useless because the bathroom used hand-drying machines.

Toilet paper would have to do. I soaked it with soap and water and began to scrub, but to no avail. All I had managed to do was to smear all the makeup together and make a hideous design on my shoulder. Come to think of it, though, the design was a lot cuter than some of the designs I'd seen in the department stores. That's what I had to tell myself anyway, for I was due back on the platform to speak at the women's luncheon.

With no time to cover my mess, I walked up before five hundred women. Every third person stopped me to ask if I knew there was something on my shoulder. Trying to make a joke out of it, I replied, "Oh, no! You've got to be kidding!" and feigned horror at the mess on my breast.

Despite the stain, what followed was indescribable. The Spirit of God moved through that horrid stain and what it represented. As I began to explain the obvious to the crowd, I began to weep. As the words tumbled out, tears tumbled down, and several women were dabbing at their eyes with ratty Kleenex (you know, the sort of tissue that gets left in the bottom of your purse, only to be brought out in a desperate moment). The sweet sound of tears. So precious to God, so lovely, the tears of a righteous woman. He bottles them all.

It was not a display of self-pity, but a spontaneous healing service authored by the Holy Spirit. I have never been in a meeting like it since. It was wonderful to see the Lord pour out His Spirit in such a sovereign manner with incredible love. That is the only way I can describe it, and even that falls short. All that would come out of me were the words, "Jesus, Jesus."

It brought to mind the verse that mentions One whose "name is ointment poured forth" (Song 1:3). The Balm of Gilead was there, and words seemed useless. To speak would break the reverence of His presence. Who were we, that He would show up after we had such a well-planned itinerary to invoke His presence? He didn't even need it. He saw the desire. He saw the hearts of His women who had gathered, not to hear another roster of speakers, each trying to do a little better than the last. They had gathered for the simple purpose of having what we were experiencing then. Right in the middle of our agenda.

A Holy Visitation

In my lifetime, I have known only what it is to *have* electricity. Believe me when I tell you that I have traveled to many foreign countries that did not have electricity. I did not realize how I took electricity for granted until a local pastor in the Philippines found me wandering about the hut, looking for a place to plug in my curling iron. What a wuss!

Years ago, women would wash the family clothes in a tub and beat them with a stick to thrash out the dirt left from the soapy water. There was no air-conditioning, no lights, only candles. There was no electricity, and no switch to turn it on.

The trolleys, or streetcars, that are such a novelty today had no power of their own. Though they had motors, the motors were not like the bus engines of today. The power to make those motors run was in the power lines above them.

Streetcars are still used in some areas today, most often in Europe. What is so ironic is that a streetcar carrying seventy-five people up a steep hill can outdo a struggling car in second or third gear chugging up the same hill. The streetcar just glides past, yet it has no power of its own. There are no gears. It has a trolley, its overhead mechanism, that touches electrified power lines overhead. When the trolley touches those electric lines, the power moves the seventy-five people up the hill with no effort.

My husband, Randi, and I once took a train trip from London to North Wales. For part of the trip, we went on an electrified train. Those carriages can go 120 miles per hour. There is a great monster at the front, and behind it are a dozen or more carriages. There is no power in those carriages. They must be "coupled up" to the first locomotive. Then as long as that first locomotive is in touch with the electric system, all the cars will run at top speed.

This is true of anything that is run by electricity. You can push a lawn mower, or you can plug it in. I can cut my grass at home with no effort because I have an electric lawn mower. (Actually I have never mowed my lawn, but I have stood at the window and yelled excellent instructions to the lawn guy.) Screwdrivers, stoves, heaters, irons, washing machines, dryers—everything is now powered by electricity. We don't have to sweat anymore. All we have to do is to turn on the switch.

I don't know of anything as much like the power of God as electricity.

Where Is the Power?

In a sense, electricity is like the very power of God. It brings life to things that were dead. Moses declared that he needed the presence of God and God's glory to go with him. Who wants a destiny without God in it? Even so, I am in approximately fifty churches every year, and while I see a hunger for the power of God, I don't really see the electricity that I know He has for us.

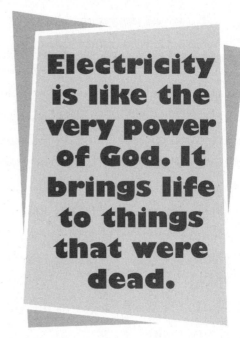

Electricity is like the very power of God. It brings life to things that were dead.

Not by might nor by power, but by my Spirit. (Zech. 4:6 NIV)

If the Spirit of him that raised Jesus up from the dead dwell in you, he shall electrify you. (Rom. 8:11)

So how do we become electrified? In much the same way as electric irons, alarm clocks, or anything with a plug. Plug in and turn on the switch. It's that simple. You plug yourself into your power source, flip the switch, and the power flows.

Jesus said, "I can of My own self do nothing" (John 5:19, author's paraphrase). Jesus is our divine prototype. To my utter amazement, I see that the prototype has no power at all. He was showing us a divine principle.

But we are clogged up, blocked with so much knowledge. We have books and tapes and sermon notes—all designed to teach us "how to do it." We search for power from other, independent sources rather than from God. But these have made us the enemies of God because He will not share His glory with anyone (Isa. 48:11).

When we plug in and nothing happens, we have a short circuit somewhere. Romans 11:36 (KJV) tells us, "Of him, and through him, and to him, are all things: to whom be glory for ever." Look at the prepositions in this passage: *of, through, to*. The circuit should flow *from* Him, *through* me, and then back *to* Him. But the moment I believe that there is anything that originates in *me*, then I have a short circuit, and the glory stops.

God Himself safeguards the glory. Why? Because all credit, all glory, is due *His* name.

God is the originator of the current. His Spirit is the electricity that sends everything into motion. It moves, it generates, it heats, it gives light, it gives revelation, it gives power, it gives health, and it gives quickening. Everything is by the Spirit of God. We must recognize that.

"Whatever You Do, Don't Touch That"

My parents moved our family into a 120-year-old house. It was the only place available to rent when they moved to plant a new church work. You know those quaint old homes from the turn of the century that are featured in *Southern Homes* and *House Beautiful*? The ones with lovely wooden floors and a grand mahogany staircase? Well, this house was *not* one of those.

Think of the house from the old sitcom *The Real McCoys* or the house from *The Beverly Hillbillies* . . . the one they moved out of. This house had a ratio of one person to every twelve hundred rats. And I hate rats.

As a gift to my mother, an electrician-plumber in our church put in a bathroom for us. He did everything but wire the vanity mirror above the sink. My father did that.

Now, my father was the dearest, kindest soul who ever dropped onto this planet, and his heart was right. Unfortunately sometimes his projects were just a little . . . well . . . they didn't work quite the way they should have. He meant well.

One day we heard a piercing scream and ran upstairs toward the sound. My mother appeared at the door of her newly minted bathroom, bug-eyed, her red hair on end, and wearing the most horrified expression I had witnessed in all of my ten years.

It seems that my dear father had wired the light over the mirror in such a way that if one touched the mirror and the bathroom faucet at the same time, she received an electric shock that made her think she was on death row. And because Daddy did not know how he created the phenomenon, he didn't know how to fix it, so the problem continued, and we got used to it. It got to the point that no one even moved if we heard a scream. We nonchalantly said, "Don't worry. Someone just got electrocuted on the sink." I figured everyone's sink and mirror worked like that.

It wouldn't surprise me to learn that one of our distant relatives was healed of a heart murmur during a summer visit. Not a bad idea. Why pay for expensive heart surgery when you could just touch the Rotherts' mirror?

Some houses have a fuse box. It is very specifically made. It uses a five-amp fuse (aren't you impressed that I knew that?), which is a delicate little wire. If anything blows, the fuse blows. And it is easier to replace a fuse than to build another house because it burned down.

God is heaven's great electrician, and all power is His. That power is His glory, and His glory is His. Just as an electrician is concerned about the building not burning down, God, in turn, is concerned about His glory. Once He sees a man wanting to take glory and honor for himself that is rightfully God's, then that man is in danger. God will not allow that.

When those who are gifted in ministry, who are serving God, deliberately choose to take the glory that is rightfully God's alone for themselves, or they ignore God's glory and holiness and with carelessness and disdain "trample underfoot" that glory, they put themselves and those around them in jeopardy.

Letting It Flow Through Us

One night my husband and I were watching a Christian television show. A most amazing singer was leading worship. Both of us remarked on the gift and anointing he possessed. I casually asked what had happened to the other fellow who used to lead such lovely worship on that program. Then I remembered that he had fallen into moral failure, been humiliated before the entire country, and wound up losing his ministry and his family.

My husband turned to me and said, "Honey, never forget that

God always has plenty of people waiting in the wings to take your place should you fail Him."

His words hit me like a ton of bricks. I knew, of course, that they were true, but I did not like the prospect of being so easily replaced. Understanding God's incredible love for me is a no-brainer, but the ditches are littered with men and women who once had an awesome anointing and didn't even realize when it was gone. May God help us!

In the pursuit of my destiny, I will come to the place of touching the electricity of His anointing. Will I allow it to flow through me, then back to Him, and give Him all the glory? Or will I take credit for what comes into my hands and then short-circuit His life in me? ("I know it was God who healed them, but it was *my* hand that touched them," that sort of thing.) Am I willing to pay the price for one dear soul? Will I give my shoulder for a person whom I might never meet again, someone who will, in all likelihood, mess up my suit? One individual was worth all the blood spilled at the cross. That is the mystery of redemption.

Messages on destiny usually stir up your flesh, but if that is all they do, they are no

> **In the pursuit of my destiny, I will come to the place of touching the electricity of His anointing.**

better than Abu Dabu's self-help manual that he received on the top of the mountain in Mylapersia.

No, my friend, this is a message of hope, of finding life by the willingness to die. My destiny comes as I am willing to *lay down* my destiny.

What about you? Are you willing to spend your whole life loving and serving that man you married? If not, then for what are you willing to give your whole life?

If you listen to the popular voices of TV today, they will tell you: "Don't lay down your life for anyone or anything. You owe it to yourself to pursue *your* dream." That message breeds selfishness.

At times, we even use the Scriptures for building our own kingdoms. Please understand that I love the passages that promise household salvation, healing, and prosperity, but I am becoming more and more aware of the simple message of God's saving love to a very terrifying world.

Do you want to know what happened to that dear woman who cried all over my suit? She was a pastor's wife who had found out the night before that her husband of more than twenty years had committed adultery with her best friend. She wanted to divorce him and leave the ministry. Was there hope for her? That was the question in her heart as she came seeking answers at the book table in the foyer of the church.

It has been more than five years since all that happened. She and her husband are together, they have a new baby, and their ministry has grown. God has used them in reconciling many marriages and families, and in bringing to salvation many lost souls.

Is any destiny better than that? I'll give you a dollar if you can prove it. No, better make that two dollars. The kids' lunch money is due tomorrow.

Chapter Thirteen

Heaven's My Home, but Earth Is Month to Month

The old saying, "They are so heavenly minded that they are no earthly good," may be true at times for different individuals, but I think it all depends on what image we have of heaven.

If you think that heaven is all about sitting around in a white La-Z-Boy recliner and watching Christian television with Gabriel and Peter, then eternity is really going to be a long time.

The heaven I perceive is one of great activity. According to the Word of God, thousands upon ten thousands of people from every tribe, nation, tongue, and color will be crowding around the throne for their opportunity to give praise to the Lamb.

Many of us will feel that our praise and thanks are more appreciated than those of any others. I know it will take me hundreds of years just to get through thanking Him for my teenage years alone.

What I desire to convey in this chapter are some living principles. These are principles that *live*. But in turn, they are also principles to live *by*.

This past weekend I went out to minister at a church, accompanied by a dear friend, first in a conference setting, then at the sponsoring church itself. From the moment we were picked up at the airport, I had a sinking feeling that all was not well. The gentleman who greeted us let me know that having "airport duty" was distasteful and a bother to his already full schedule. Every mile or so we were reminded that he had other quite pressing ministerial duties, none of which involved us, thank you very much.

Nice Outfit—Too Bad They Didn't Have It in Your Size

When I walked into the first service, I could feel the eyes of the pastor's wife boring a hole in me. At first I thought I was just being oversensitive. *Come on, Cathy, this is ridiculous. Why wouldn't she like you? She doesn't even know you,* I tried to reason within myself. After the first two services, it was apparent even to my traveling companion (she is my armor bearer, my chief intercessor, my best friend, and my encourager from God).

"Gee, Cathy, I don't think the pastor's wife likes you. Maybe she thinks your dress is too short or the pants you wore yesterday were too tight . . . or maybe it's your hair."

I told her she could stop encouraging me anytime now.

But the power of God had been demonstrated to His people in the meeting, so I thought that if the pastor's wife had any reservations about the ministry, hearing me speak and watching the demonstration of the Holy Spirit would turn her around.

Instead, she was alienated from me even more. It was difficult to preach with a passion to a thousand people only to look over and see the pastor's wife with her hand over her mouth, whispering to the other guest speaker sitting beside her. Every now and then, the two would nod and smile at each other in my direction. *Unnerving. Rude. Immature.* All these thoughts were running through my brain, while something totally different was coming out of my mouth.

> **The power of God had been demonstrated to His people in the meeting.**

I was trying to teach on the power of forgiveness, the commandments of love, and the requirements of being a container of His glory. While my message was correct, I'm afraid my heart was not. It got worse.

The pastor's wife was taking us back to the hotel when she turned to me and said, "We are releasing you from the rest of the meeting. We perceive that you are too ill to continue." It did not matter how much I tried to convince her that I was not ill. Her mind had been made up since the first service. I begged her to tell me if I had in any way offended her. She assured me that was not the case. Minutes later, I stood in the driveway of the hotel, briefcase and purse in hand, and watched her drive away, leaving me feeling desolate.

Later that day we saw the same woman having lunch with the

other guest speaker and the senior pastor. They were laughing and eating, my two favorite things in the whole world. And there I stood, looking like an orphan with no food. I felt like the kid who didn't get picked for the team. Just before I slithered out, she saw me. I waited for a gesture to come and join them, but all I got was a half smile.

For the next three hours I rehearsed the conversation and events in my mind. What could be done? What had *I* done? *I'll call her. No, I'll just tell everyone I know that she used to be a Playboy Bunny.* No, I couldn't do that. She wasn't cute enough.

Never Let Your Methods Invalidate Your Message

I was miserable. What would she say to all the people who were coming to hear me minister that night and the next day? Would it paint me in a bad light? How could I communicate to the congregation that I really wanted to be there, that it wasn't my fault?

I couldn't, and that bugged me. There was absolutely nothing left to do but leave. I began to mutter my dismay as I threw every piece of clothing back into my suitcase. "It's not fair. I won't even get to wear my chocolate leather jacket." I was not used to being asked to leave. My pride was hurt, and my dignity was wounded. It wasn't until I laid my head on the pillow that night that the Holy Spirit spoke to me.

Cathy, if you allow your methods to become louder than your message, your ministry will be invalidated.

Huh? I scrambled out of bed in search of a pen and paper to write down what I felt the Lord had spoken to me. It is always a marvelous thing to hear God speak at any time, but when He speaks during a time of trouble, it is especially important and meaningful. I did not want to lose this one. I was being told that my methods, my ways of doing things, my behavior, and my words spoken in haste or in an unkind manner speak so loudly that they have the power of wiping out my wonderful message. So no matter what someone else does, I am held to a higher standard. I must respond the way the Word of God tells me to or my ministry will be ineffective.

The few people who may not have a personal relationship with you or anyone close to you might think you walk on water; however, those who truly know you, behind the scenes, will eventually speak up and share your little indiscretions, possibly your rude attitude, or even your love of gossip. Then your goose is cooked.

> No matter what someone else does, I am held to a higher standard. I must respond the way the Word of God tells me to.

It was a test, and I was failing miserably. There was still a secret spirit of pride in my heart that wanted everyone to love me and congratulate me. Ugh! How horrible it can be when God, our

Father, peels back the flesh to give us a real good glimpse of what is actually in us.

It didn't help matters any when I arrived home the next day and everyone asked me what happened. Each one tried to help me by pointing out certain character flaws that might have caused me to be kicked out of the conference. That wasn't much comfort.

Later that night, my bishop called me because he had heard what happened to me. "Well, daughter, how did it make you feel? Are you angry?" He genuinely wanted to know.

"I was angry, Bishop. I was hurt, and then I was mad. But now I'm just embarrassed. No, I'm more like humiliated."

"That's the answer I wanted to hear, daughter. It is humiliating to go through something like that when you are accustomed to being honored. But now you need to rejoice. Do you know what comes next?"

"No, sir . . . maybe death because I'm never going to leave my house again. I'll stay inside. All I really need is my muumuu and some Pepsi," I whined into the telephone.

"Honor, Cathy. God is preparing you to be greatly honored. Humility comes before honor. You must endure the humiliation, or you will never have the honor."

After I pondered that a moment, the truth of his statement dawned on me. I thanked him profusely. Those few words literally lifted the spirit of failure off me.

The enemy, who is the accuser of the brethren, does not play fair. He will accuse others to you, and then he will accuse you to yourself. If you begin to entertain those thoughts, you will be defeated. I had allowed the devil to sow the seeds of accusation in my heart and in my mind, and it had taken only three days for him to acquire a foothold in my heart.

React or Respond?

No matter what your first *reaction* is to a troubling situation, you can control your *response* to the attack afterward. That, my precious friend, is the difference between the overcomer and the joyless Christian. Joyless Christians are those who react with great emotion to any challenge presented by the enemy or people who create strife. They never learn the secret of rolling off those hurts or that anger to the Lord.

David wrote that God would hide us in His pavilion from the strife of tongues (Ps. 31:20). There is actually a place in God where we can hide from the arguing, gossip, and strife, a place inhabited by the peace of God that shields us emotionally from the contentious words that try to take hold of us and make us their slaves every day.

> No matter what your first reaction is to a troubling situation, you can control your response to the attack afterward.

I refuse to be a slave to hurt and bitterness. Bitter people are really miserable to be around. They have such sad stories, and about the four-hundredth time you hear one, you are ready to set yourself on fire. (It would be a sin to set *them* on fire, so you have to settle for yourself.) Bitterness has the ability to steal your joy. A hurt and bitter person might not readily admit it, but what he or she really wants is revenge. Yep, revenge—that individual desire to see the one who inflicted the perceived wound paid back in a small measure for all the suffering he or she caused.

The truth is, you still wouldn't be happy even if revenge were enacted upon your enemies. You cannot please a demon. The same spirit that sowed the hurt will constantly remind you of all the people who have wounded you until your methods render your message useless. That is exactly what the enemy desires: to render you harmless and useless.

Please allow me to take you on a little side trip to share with you a few of the nuggets and living principles that God has been teaching me so that I don't invalidate my ministry. I believe they will help you as well on your journey.

Trusting the Father

Let's begin with an obscure story in 2 Chronicles 14. King Asa, the main character in this story, was a man who truly loved God. His desire to please Him caused him to tear down all the heathen altars that had been built by his forefathers. Though the altars represented thousands of dollars, Asa did not care. The altars had been used in the past for sacrifices to false gods, and that really offended the Father. Asa loved the Father so much that he went against public opinion and removed the symbols of idolatry, cutting down the wooden images and breaking the sacred pillars.

As a result, God was pleased with Asa and gave him peace and rest. There was no war in those years. That is truly amazing. The favor of God was upon the king and the kingdom to such a degree that no one dared to attack him. Until . . .

Asa turned right around and did something dumb. Though the land was at rest, he built walls around his cities, *just in case*. He had never needed walls before. But his action indicated that he believed he would be attacked. Sure enough, Zerah the Ethiopian came out against him with a million-man army and three hundred chariots. And though Asa's army was pretty impressive—580,000 strong—his enemy outnumbered him almost two to one.

Notice how things had changed. Asa was no longer relying on God alone, which is God's perfect will. Instead, Asa placed his trust in God *and* the fortified cities *and* the great army. Even with the highest favor of God, Asa had allowed fear to motivate him to prepare for war. He slowly began to depend less on God and more on the things he could see. Consequently, instead of growing in faith, he began to grow in fear.

Facing the reality of being wiped out and conquered by an ungodly king and his army, Asa did what all of us have done through the years: he cried out to God. I love the prayer that King Asa prayed. Can you imagine? Standing there in the middle of the Valley of Zephathah, he cried out:

LORD, it is nothing for You to help, whether with many or with those who have no power; help us, O LORD our God, for we rest on You, and in Your name we go against this multitude. O LORD, You are our God; do not let this man prevail against You! (2 Chron. 14:11)

What an incredible prayer, filled with compliments to God and humility from the king.

It worked because God did come to Asa's aid, and he crushed the Ethiopians. What a battle it was. But now it was over.

The temptation after any battle is to let down our guards because we are sick and tired of the stinkin' war. We just want peace and a massage. But God needed to say a few things to Asa, such as, "I pulled your sorry self out of the fire this time, buddy, but you forsake Me again, and I will forsake

> **Help us, O Lord our God, for we rest on You.**

you." So God sent a prophet to Asa, who delivered both a warning and encouragement.

The next chapter confuses me a little. (It doesn't take much to do that sometimes.) In 2 Chronicles 15:8, the Word tells us that after Asa heard the word of the Lord from the prophet, he had the courage to remove the idols from the land. Now, didn't Asa already do that in chapter 14? Hadn't he "cut down the wooden images"? I mean, where was I? Maybe while Asa was busy building his army and his walls, certain people were rebuilding the idols. Or maybe he did only *half* the job of removing idolatry from his kingdom.

This story shows me that we need to be continually on our faces before the Father. Human nature has a tremendous capability to forget. I never understood how men or women who were used of

God in remarkable ways could turn around and sin and betray their faith. But then, sin is much like a weed.

In the Garden

Last summer I got the brilliant idea of planting a garden. I thought about how nice it would be to hear my children ask for dinner, followed by my grabbing a little basket and going to my backyard. There I would pick fresh vegetables with my bare hands. Fresh green beans; plump, juicy red tomatoes that had not been gassed in a warehouse somewhere; tender greens, a fresh salad made from my own Bibb lettuce; radishes with the dirt still on them; and spring onions that had taste to them.

My secretary and I went to Home Depot and bought a shovel, a spade, a wheelbarrow, soaking hoses, fertilizer, and packets of seeds. We spent five hundred dollars that day. It felt so good digging the plot of ground, turning over the dirt, and putting the little seeds in the ground.

We made little Popsicle-stick signs. Then we went back to Home Depot and purchased little pots of already growing vegetables. I wasn't cheating, I told myself. I just needed a little help against the elements. I spent another seventy-five dollars that day. For the next few weeks we would go out three times a day and have a look.

My first crop consisted of one bell pepper about two inches high (I had to harvest it because wild creatures were starting to eat it), three carrots, a radish, and the smallest head of lettuce I have ever seen. I thought we could take a picture of it for the *Guinness Book of Records*. You know the guy who has the largest pumpkin in the world? I could stand next to him with the smallest head of lettuce ever recorded.

Someone told us that we needed a row of yellow marigolds and a nice organic fertilizer. So back to Home Depot we went to pick up a couple of cans of fertilizer and a few more tomato plants because little worm things ate ours. We also purchased ten tomato cages by faith that the tomato plants would yield dozens of plump, red, juicy fruits. My total at the checkout that day was ninety-six dollars and change.

I am now the proud owner of a slightly used wheelbarrow, a hoe, a spade, half a bag of leftover dirt, and ten brand-new tomato cages. I still believe that I can make the *Guinness Book of Records,* but under a new category: the fattest garden worms in the world.

It really takes diligence to keep out the bugs.

Eventually my labor paid off. I harvested two more peppers, four—can you believe it?—radishes, and one ear of corn. Guinness wants me for a new category now: the most money ever spent for a backyard garden. I added up my expenses that September and then divided them by the number of vegetables without any worm holes. It seems I spent around $367.52 per vegetable.

Jesus often compared Himself to the farmer and His Word to the seed. Jesus said we are the field the seed falls into. Can you

imagine the great difficulty the farmer, Jesus, has in getting anything to grow in us? We are even warned that as soon as the seed
is dropped into our hearts, the enemy comes along to steal it.
Everything is set to destroy the hope that has been deposited
inside you.

But we are told that if we seek Him with all of our hearts, He
will bring that seed to fruition. What is fruition? It is seeing with
your own eyes the fulfillment of every promise that God has
dropped into your heart. However, it really takes diligence to keep
out the bugs.

Asa Really Blew It

It doesn't matter that you did all the right things in the past. If you
stop doing them in this season, it doesn't take long for the bugs to
move in. That is why Asa had to go back to the high places and
remove idols again. Not only had he failed to completely remove
idolatry in his first campaign against it, but most likely the "ver-
min" moved in and rebuilt what he had destroyed before.

Asa recommitted himself and the people to the Lord and sealed
it with a huge sacrifice. All the people shouted and sang and
jumped around. They were really serious this time. They even
swore that whoever would not seek the Lord, be it man, woman,
or child, would be put to death (2 Chron. 15:13).

The next part is really funny, but then I also have a slightly warped
sense of humor. One of Asa's most serious actions was to remove his
mother (that's right, his mother) from the honor of being queen
mother because she had built a perverted image of the goddess
Asherah. Her son stood up to her by cutting the idol down, burning

it, and removing her from a place of authority. I'm not sure, but I bet she was really mad at him!

It is necessary at times to stand up to your own family without the fear of rejection. Because Asa did so, God honored him and gave him thirty-five years of peace.

In year thirty-six, another king rose up against Asa. You would think by then that Asa would have learned his lesson and would have immediately cried out to the Lord to save him as he had been instructed. But *nooooo!* Instead he hatched a plan to bribe a third party to become an ally with him, using as payment silver and gold from the house of the Lord.

It's really easy for me to sit here in my daughter's bedroom in front of a typewriter and criticize Asa. But the truth is that all of us are prone to lean on our own understanding. We pride ourselves on figuring out our own destinies and then deciding how to get there. Then we spend the rest of our lives cleaning up the messes we made and being mad at God for allowing us to have our own way.

It was a small test, yet Asa failed miserably. He almost got away with it, too, except that God always honors His promises. The Lord sent a prophet to tell Asa that he had done wrong and that the Lord's protection would be lifted. Asa would have the very thing he had tried all those years to avoid: war. The king was so angry that he had the prophet thrown into prison.

Suddenly Asa developed a very nasty foot problem. The Bible tells us that Asa would not humble himself to call upon the Lord, but turned only to his doctors. Within five years of his turning to the king of Syria for help, Asa was dead. He had been warned. It is always sad to see someone who carried such authority and did so many great things for God make a stupid decision that ruins everything.

Principles for Protection

How can you protect yourself from the thing that destroyed King Asa and so many others down through the centuries?

Principle #1: If you seek God and keep seeking Him, He has promised to be found by you. He is a kind, benevolent God who is not mad at you. Many people never turn to God in time of trouble because they think that it is wrong to seek Him only when they need something. Well, that is basically true; however, God is standing at the ready. Just ask Him.

Principle #2: Keep your garden weeded. Satan's favorite ways to ravage your garden? Pride, self-reliance, rejection, and fear of what others think, including but not limited to your mother.

Principle #3: Having money can be a great blessing, but it does not hold all the answers. I know many Christians who make all their decisions based on the balances in their checkbooks. They are never really financially blessed because of it. If Asa had not had the money to bribe the king of Syria, he would have had to cry out to God for help. Sometimes money causes more trouble than it solves.

Principle #4: Never make decisions without first seeking God's face. Rely on Him. Wait on Him. Rest in Him.

Principle #5: This will be one of the best pieces of advice you will ever receive. I foresee thousands of people sending me a lot of money for this bit of life-changing counsel: never—raise your right hand and say this with me—ever decide in a weak moment to put in a vegetable garden unless you are a farmer. If you are tempted to do this, I will tell you how to get free from the nagging, persistent voice that says, "Gee, how hard can it be? A few seeds, some dirt . . ." Go outside to where you are tempted to plant your garden and open your wallet. Now take out a one-hundred-dollar bill, light a match, and set fire to your money. Watch it burn. That, my dear friend, is what will happen if you do not listen to me.

If you still insist that you are the exception and I'm just a dumb blonde who did not know what she was doing, write to me and I will sell you some slightly used gardening equipment and ten brand-new tomato cages. There will be no charge for the worms.

Chapter Fourteen

In Case of Emergency, Reach for Chocolate

Once a month I get an overwhelming need for a couple of those milk cartons of malted milk balls. I *love* them! I also love that Belgian-made Godiva chocolate. White chocolate is the best. I can eat a lot of it, and no one sees it on my face.

One of my very favorite childhood memories is of my mother buying me a white chocolate Easter bunny. First I ate out the candy eyes, and then I bit off its chocolate head. Well, I'm forty-six years old, and Mom still buys me that bunny every year along with yellow marshmallow Peeps. Thanks, Mom!

Randi and I have five daughters and two sons. I also employ three women to help out in the house and with the children on occasion. Two of the women are full-time, and one is part-time. Counting all the females in the house, there are quite a few hormones. I have found that when women live and work with one another, they tend to also "cycle" around one another. That is very scary news for any men who work with or around these women. So . . . my husband has asked me to please give him a heads-up when all of us are on our cycles.

One month I asked my husband do this when he came home: come to the front door, ring the doorbell, open the door, throw in some chocolate, and slam the door quickly. After he heard the sounds of lions' growls die down, then it was safe to open the door.

In premise, he opens the door and there we stand, all of us women and our hormones, with chocolate all over our faces . . . but content. I read somewhere, probably in *Women and Chocolate* magazine, that chocolate contains some sort of vitamin or mineral, and without it on a daily basis, you will die. (Okay, I made up the part about dying.)

Each of my friends has some sort of comfort food that helps her get through the darkest nights. The only problem is, unless your comfort food is celery, you will just trade one problem for another. You are free to eat twelve Hershey's candy bars (I prefer Reese's Peanut Butter Cups) whenever you wish. You are also free to buy size thirty-two wide pants, which is what I needed at my top weight.

Answers That Prevail

I have an answer that will comfort you in times of trouble *without* making you morbidly obese. Most people cringe when they hear it, though. All the feelings of failure that they have ever had come crashing back, and they turn off rather than face another humiliation. But this answer I propose is a secret weapon to use in any situation, great or small. What is that secret weapon? *Prayer.*

I beg you not to skip this. I promise I will not beat you up or make you feel guilty, and when you finish this chapter, you will not be able to wait any longer to pray.

A book on destiny would not be complete without a chapter on prayer. Prayer separates this book from other self-help books on the market. Believe me, there are thousands. If they all worked, there would be no need for more self-help books. But it is not enough to tell someone that she needs to change. We all know that. Instead we must be equipped with the tools to *facilitate* our change. Prayer is a tool. And without banging you over the head with the Bible, I long to give you the impetus to pray.

As a teenager, I read a book that so changed my life concerning prayer that I made it required reading for all those who attend my mentoring class. That book is *Reese Howell, Intercessor.* The author was a man who did not *talk* about praying; he really prayed.

> I propose a secret weapon to use in any situation, great or small: Prayer.

Many are the prayer meetings I have attended where folks took the first hour and a half talking *about* prayer needs, but then prayed only fifteen minutes. I left those meetings feeling guilty. But as I read about the life of Reese Howell, I had to lay prostrate on the floor. I could not go low enough. I remember thinking, *If I ever write a book, I want it to have this kind of impact on others*. I was very surprised to find out that I was not the only person to have discovered this treasure of prayer. That book was actually a Christian classic. Here I thought it was my personal revelation.

Prayer is bringing your needs, petitions, and desires to the Lord. I liken it to the ability to bypass the layers of bureaucracy and go straight to the president of the company. Who hasn't spent time on the telephone talking to people who have no ability to help? Prayer puts you in direct contact with the One who can make things happen.

As a ten-year-old child, I began to feel very tired all the time. My arms ached and my legs were cramping, but mostly I was just lethargic. Though a tomboy, I no longer had the energy to play the usual baseball and army soldiers after school.

My parents made a doctor's appointment for me, much to my surprise. I can count on one hand the times my parents had to take us to the doctor. If one of us kids woke up on a school morning complaining about some malady, my mom always had the same answer: "Get up and get dressed. You'll feel better when you get to school." Unless I was holding my severed head in my hands, there was no reason to stay home from school.

In those days, the mid-sixties, the nurse would draw blood and put it on a little flat piece of glass. That is what they did at the doctor's that day. It seemed as though we were in his office for hours. I was only ten, and anything more than fifteen minutes felt like an eternity.

I vividly remember my mother standing in front of the doctor's desk as he talked in a hushed tone. Then she took out her church hankie—the white one with the crocheted lace in graduated shades of purple—and wiped tears from her eyes. I had never seen my mother cry. Well, not exactly true. When I was five years old, I came home from school and heard crying coming from her bedroom. My father came from behind me and quietly said, "Your mommy is crying because her daddy just died." I wasn't as moved by my grandfather's death as I was by the sight of my mother crying. Now she was crying again, and I wanted to comfort her. I really wanted her to stop because she was freaking me out.

The next morning, accompanied by both parents, I went to the hospital. I was excited because, not only did I get to skip school, but I had both parents all to myself, and they were being especially sweet and paying me a lot of attention.

More blood, more little pieces of glass. I barely had the strength to eat the ice-cream cone they bought for me at the Whistle Stop, an ice-cream stand down by the railroad tracks. My brothers and I routinely begged my father after every Sunday and Wednesday night church service to take us to the Whistle Stop, but usually we didn't go.

Now we were having ice cream in the middle of the day on a Wednesday. Something was wrong, but I didn't care, I had an ice-cream cone. I should have cared. I was dying. The doctor called my parents that night during supper. My mom took the call and looked gravely at my dad as she replaced the receiver.

Isn't it funny the things you remember during life's important moments? That was truly a night that changed all of our lives, but what I remember are the smells of the kitchen. We had corned beef hash with tomatoes that night. I can still see my mother holding the receiver of that big black phone, a white apron covering a pink-and-white gingham shirtwaist. My folks sat me on the couch and told me with the bravest faces they could muster that we were going to pack a little suitcase for me because I was going back to the hospital the next day.

I was thrilled. Another missed school day, another whole day with my parents, and the thought of another ice cream. Being a parent now, I can only imagine the terror my parents were facing. There were no bone marrow transplants, no chemotherapy. I had leukemia, and the most my parents could hope for was that I might be with them for six months.

My parents pastored our church, and midweek services were on Wednesday nights. I wouldn't be going (*yippee!*), but I found out later that it was a service unlike any ever seen in that church before.

> **They were struck by the intensity of God's presence.**

That evening, after sharing my diagnosis with the choir during their pre-service practice, my parents called the choir members to pray. Then as others began drifting into the church expecting the usual Wednesday night crowd and midweek teaching, they were struck by the intensity of God's presence. The choir had gathered at the altar on their knees, crying out to God. Rather than stopping to share the need, people quietly slipped to the front to join their voices with the others. That night there was an urgency—a child's life was in the balance, the doctors had no answers, and it was up to them to cry out and petition heaven for a miracle.

Those People Could Really Pray

My family was always very private, and my parents drilled into us kids *never* to talk about the things that happened in our family. For my parents to open up and share such private news in a community that sat in the heart of Amish country was truly humbling. But sometimes it is natural to share very intimate things with people who can pray. And my father knew *those* church members could pray. We needed a miracle, so the church bombarded the gates of heaven for it.

Why do some people get their miracles, while others don't? I don't pretend to know the answer. The great Kathryn Kuhlman was asked that same question, and she had no answer either. What I do know is that if you don't pray, you deny yourself the opportunity of gaining God's assistance. Would you really want to do this thing called life without it?

We went to the hospital the next morning. I had a new set of baby doll pajamas bought especially for the trip, and I sat

> **There is nothing like a miracle to begin to turn up the fire and the faith of God's people.**

on the bed with my parents by my side while I faced a new round of tests. Once again, more blood, more glass slides, nurses and their aides coming in and out of the room. This is sort of embarrassing to admit, but since I didn't understand the extent of my illness, I actually was enjoying being the center of attention.

The end came as quickly as it began. No, I didn't die. It doesn't mean that the enemy did not try to take my life then and on several other occasions, but my days are in the hands of the Lord. The doctor had come in earlier than usual that morning. He took my parents out in the hallway to talk. They came back in together, doctors and nurses accompanied by members of my family. The mood was jubilant, and my father sat on the bed beside me and said, "Cathy, get up, honey. We're going home."

It seems that the last two sets of blood work had seen a miraculous change in the white blood cell count. It seems that in twenty-four hours I went from being deathly ill with leukemia to perfectly healthy and normal. Well, I don't know about the normal part. That was at least fifteen years ago (ha ha), and neither the disease nor its symptoms have ever returned.

Can you imagine the church service we had the next Sunday? Not only did the people rejoice in what God had done for me, but their faith was bolstered to believe God for circumstances in their own lives. *There is nothing like a miracle to begin to turn up the fire and the faith of God's people.*

I'm Just So Busy

Believe me, I understand when people tell me that they are so busy, it is hard to find time to pray. Everyone is busy. But prayer is the weapon God gave to us to help bring about change. Furthermore, in Luke 18:1, Jesus told us that if we do not pray, we will lose heart.

Then He went on to tell an interesting story about an ungodly man who was a judge. A woman, a nobody really, a nothing, came to appeal her case to the ungodly judge, who just blew her off. But the widow had nothing to lose, and the judge was her last hope. He finally was exasperated by her, and out of sheer selfishness for his own peace and quiet he granted her justice: "And shall God not avenge His own elect who cry out day and night to Him, though He bears long with them? I tell you that He will avenge them speedily" (Luke 18:7–8).

Life has ways of keeping us so busy that even with the best intentions we never get around to prayer. Who has not set the alarm clock for 5:00 A.M., fully intending to roll out of bed and pray for an hour, only to start pushing the snooze button for just ten more minutes? Pretty soon it's 8:15, you're late for work, the kids have missed the bus, and you're trying to pray while roaring down the interstate.

That night you crawl into bed with your Bible, fully intending to read a little from the Psalms, some of Proverbs, followed by a chapter or two from the Gospels, only to fall asleep while adjusting your pillow to begin reading.

In my house there is only one more thing to do before I start praying. Thinking that I can multitask my spiritual life, I throw a load of clothes in the washer, take a chicken out of the freezer to defrost, return a couple of phone calls—all of this so that I won't be interrupted when I finally get down to prayer. Except that then the clothes have finished washing, so I need to throw them in the dryer, and I might as well throw in another load to wash.

Then the school calls with some important information that just cannot wait. One of the kids has swallowed the class goldfish, and I must immediately bring in a new one because the children are traumatized. Or they forgot their lunch, and God forbid the principal lets them eat the school lunch without paying. The school board might go under for that $2.50.

So ends another day without prayer. Allow me to let you in on a little secret. If I go one day without prayer, I can tell. If I go two days without prayer, my family can tell. If I go three, the world can tell.

Prayer Is Turning to the Living God

Prayer is the turning of the human soul to the living God (Ps. 25:1). It begins with humbling yourself, which is the only way you can come to God. My mother and father had to humble themselves and do something very distasteful for them, which was to be open in front of their congregation and admit they were battling and needed help. That is pleasing to God.

God is not an egomaniac sitting on the throne saying, "Come on, tell Me how awesome and wonderful I am. I want to hear it one more time." That He already knows who He is and that He has about a quadrillion angels to worship Him all the time *without* complaining is apparent. His purpose in wanting us to pray is to bring His heart and mind into the situation and assist us as our Father.

One of the first things a toddler learns to say is, "No! I can do it myself, Mommy." Defiantly he insists that after three years of life experience, he no longer needs the assistance of anyone, especially you. Unless he is in mortal danger, we step back and allow him to take his best shot. All the while wanting to help him we must wait until he becomes so frustrated that he finally admits he may need a *little* help.

Our Father desperately wants to assist you. Stop reciting all the reasons that you don't deserve His help and why He won't help you. He already knows you don't deserve His mercy and grace, but that is exactly why you can trust Him.

> **His purpose in wanting us to pray is to bring His heart and mind into the situation and assist us as our Father.**

Prayer Is Communion with God

Prayer is communion with God (Ps. 65:2). The closest thing here on earth to which we can compare this aspect of relationship with God is marriage. It is a union between two sometimes very different people, who may become one flesh physically, but it takes years to become one flesh in everything else. That is why many people give up and walk away from the marriage. There has been no abuse, no adultery; they divorce because of "incompatibility."

Well, isn't that what marriage is all about? I don't know any two people who were compatible to begin with. Looking through rose-colored glasses, I could be compatible with just about anybody.

The marriage covenant is about taking two very different people and building a relationship through love, prayer, and *compromise*. You build a relationship by spending time together, getting to know the other person through talking. We develop a relationship with the Father in the same way. We spend time together; we talk. Because the Father is perfect, He does not have to compromise. We are the ones who must change.

When I go into the bank to cash a check, I do not stand in front of the teller gazing into her eyes with a longing to get to know her better. I am there to get what is in her hand. We err in our relationship with the Father when we come into His presence looking only at His hand. But many Christians use prayer to get God to pay the bills, that is, to relieve the pressure of the immediate crisis in which they have found themselves.

God created us for fellowship.

God created us for fellowship. When He created Adam, the idea was that He would have somebody to walk with and talk with in the cool of the Garden. He didn't save us to serve Him; He has angels to serve Him. He longs for us to be available to come and walk with Him in the cool of the evening. He longs to listen and then comfort you with His presence.

That is prayer, not some solemn, boring, long-winded eulogy filled with a bunch of thees and thous and hithertos.

I fell in love little by little with my husband during the long coffees we would share in the restaurant after church. I might have noticed his eyes—well, quite frankly, I noticed everything, but his eyes drew me in.

There is a Hebrew word my husband taught me, *Yadah*. He says that it literally means "to know someone." Not as you know your friend or an acquaintance. That word *Yadah* is the biblical term for a sexual relationship. As in Abraham took Sarah for his wife and "knew" her. As after seventeen years of dedicated service to his Jesus, years of plenty and of want, years spent fighting for his faith and the gospel, sometimes in jail, the apostle Paul cried out, "Oh, that I might know Him." The word for "know" that Paul used there was the same as *Yadah*. God created the act of lovemaking so that the husband and the wife could come face-to-face, to see the pleasure recorded in the beloved's eyes.

A Jiminy Cricket Answer to Prayer

When I come into prayer, I begin with thanksgiving. That is not really very hard to do because I have so much to be thankful for. Like any parent, our Father wants to hear how grateful we already are for what He has done.

Not too long ago, we had all been praying as a family for God's provision to go to Disney World. Every night the children asked the Lord for the money to go to Universal Studios and to see Mickey Mouse. I was speaking in a church up North, and some dear friends of mine, Russell and Chris Fragar, had taken me out to dinner.

During dessert, Russell said that he and Chris wanted to do something for me that would be a blessing. Would it be possible, he asked, to give me two thousand dollars to take the children to Disney World? I almost fell face first into my lemon pie. Would it be all right? Jiminy Cricket—*yes!*

When I told the children what God had done for them, our prayer times got noticeably longer. The day arrived and off we went. It took three cars to load up everybody and all of our gear for an overnight trip to our destination only four hours away. We had just come off Space Mountain when my eight-year-old daughter threw her arms around me, telling me I was the best mom in the whole world and it was the best day in her entire life.

When you pray, God makes you look good. At that moment I would have done anything in the world for my child. Simply because she was grateful.

I follow my thanksgiving with praise. Sometimes I just read one of David's psalms. He put into words for me what is in my heart. After thanksgiving and praise, I am ready to bring my petitions before Him. I never bring them to the Father in a way that holds accusations of Him. Somehow I don't think that would help my cause. Rather my words are filled with faith, thanking Him before I see their fulfillment. I know He hears me, and if He hears me, I have the petition I have asked for.

Chapter Fifteen

Thighs

I read a news story some time ago that was so bizarre that at first I had trouble believing it could be true. The story revolved around a scandalous divorce caused by the wife's obsession with plastic surgery. The woman had once been a beautiful young model. But then she took drastic steps to become someone she was not. Actually it was not so much a some*one* as a some*thing*.

After her extensive surgery, her ex-husband said she looked like a panther. Now, that look on a cat is great, but not on a fiftyish woman.

Please don't misunderstand. I don't mean to knock plastic surgery. If I had an extra twenty thousand dollars sitting around, I would grab my checkbook and *run*, not walk, to the world-renowned Oriental surgeon Dr. Pinupmychin. I would follow the chin procedure by shaving off the jiggly part of my arms. You know, the part your kids grab and shake while asking you why you have thighs where your arms should be? Immediately after I Superglued each precious child's lips together, I would then have liposuction done on my thighs.

I don't know what has happened to my skin. I used to look like one of those lovely young supermodels. Okay, maybe not, but I didn't used to have so much leftover skin. And my bosom? Let's not talk about it—the subject can be so discouraging. That, of course, leads to the question, "Who is to blame? Why am I in trouble with this sagging body?"

On the eve of my forty-sixth birthday I began whining about the condition of my body. I wanted to take out a second mortgage on the house or sell our firstborn son in order to get cosmetic surgery. I spent forty-five minutes trying to sell my husband on the idea of investing in my fight against gravity. I demonstrated my little speech by pinning my thighs back, folding the skin beneath my chin into my turtleneck, and for the grand finale, pulling my face tightly backward and upward so that I looked like an alien.

Listening intently and nodding at all the right times, he waited until my little demonstration was over. I was sure I had both impressed and moved him.

"So I really think God is directing us in this matter. Don't you, honey?" Waiting for his answer, I searched his face for a sign of sympathy.

"Why don't you just exercise?" he asked.

He was so serious when he gave me his answer that it took me a second to process the ridiculous thought. That was not what I wanted to hear. I wanted *instant* transformation, not a long, drawn-out change. Almost always, change can occur when we choose to make it happen. The important thing in the matter was, whether I chose surgery or exercise, I had the ability to change.

Some Things Won't Change

From childhood we have been taught that we have the ability to change things we are not happy with. If you have straight hair but desire to look like Shirley Temple, it's easy. Just buy a Lilt perm and some little pink plastic perm rods, and in a couple of hours, if you follow directions, you can have curly hair. I've done it myself. Unfortunately my hair occasionally rebels, and instead of curls I have a massive head full of frizz.

I wanted instant transformation, not a long, drawn-out change.

Four of my daughters have coarse, ethnic hair. When the first of our daughters came into our arms, I got a crash course in styling African-American hair. I started by washing her hair every night during her bath and using a giant pick to comb it out. Every day her hair got bigger and bigger until she looked like the Michael Jackson of 1972.

After church one Sunday, some of the sisters ambushed me "in love," and their spokeswoman began the conversation by saying, "Cathy, we only say this to you because we are concerned for you.

Leave the child's hair alone." After digesting these sisters' well-intentioned information, I paid a visit to the store.

Feeling fortified with new data, I started down the hair-care aisle with a giant shopping cart. Finding the appropriate pictures of smiling little African-American girls with perfectly coifed hairstyles, I began grabbing every box, bottle, and jar that promised "easy styling with guaranteed result in minutes." Right! (Were you aware that there are approximately 297 ethnic hair-care products at Piggly Wiggly? Neither was I, but I was determined that my daughter would not suffer due to a lack of Nature's Pink Oil for Little Bitty Heads.)

Now, after four years of failing to re-create Caroline Kennedy's hairstyle on my child, I just take her to Veronica Washington's House of Beauty and Essence. I also donated forty-two boxes of hair-care kits to a grateful Veronica. That just goes to show you that there are some things in life that, no matter how hard you try, you cannot change.

Prayer Changes Things

We have been taught, and it is a true statement, that prayer changes things. I love the idea that I can stand on God's Word and see impossible situations turn around and bring God glory. We are the tools of intercession and prayer that will bring our loved ones into relationships with Jesus. What incredible power is available to us!

But what do we do when a situation presents itself, and pray as we will, nothing happens? Sometimes there are difficult challenges that simply do not respond to prayer. Or so we think.

Ladies, in our journey to fulfilling God's purposes in our lives, this is a critical issue! After all, we are serving a God for whom "nothing is impossible." But we do not get any help from our culture. Just take a look at the advertising trends today.

Our present-day advertising teaches us not to put up with anything that is the least bit distasteful . . . such as gray hair. It was out of desperation that a woman in France by the name of Madame Marie Curie ran to her backyard lab and spent days mixing viable chemicals until she finally discovered Formula #69—Champagne Blonde Hair Dye. It was only after her three strands of gray were successfully covered that she could concentrate on curing diseases with penicillin. After all, a woman must have priorities. When she went to collect her Nobel Prize, her hair looked goooood! Now any woman over fourteen years old knows that it really doesn't matter what hair color you were born with. God gave us the incredible scientific knowledge to change it.

My friend's son had his ears pinned back. Another friend got her spider veins removed. Still another had the crow's-feet around her eyes tacked up and her gullywhopper removed. (You know, it's the turkey thing that wiggles hideously under one's chin.)

We have the ability to change jobs if we want to, leave our churches, and even leave our faith if we so decide. People who pledge till death do us part (some several times over) have the option of leaving their mates if they so desire. Hate glasses? Get contacts. Always wanted blue eyes but got stuck with Aunt Clara's green ones? No problem. You can change them with colored contacts. Essentially anything about your appearance can be changed according to your own desires and timetable.

That is why it is so difficult when we are dealing with kingdom concerns and find that there are some things we cannot change even though we pray, beg, cry, and scream. Ladies, we can't change the identity of our parents even if we were adopted.

I'm So Glad You Asked

So what do we do when we know that God desires to bring a change in our circumstances, but nothing seems to happen when we pray? Do we continue to pray even if it takes forever? The answer is yes. Why? Because every time we pray, spiritual warfare is taking place. Forces unseen are working desperately to delay the answers to our prayers.

> **Every time we pray, spiritual warfare is taking place.**

So what do we do? We pray.

Then we give it up. Yes, you heard me correctly. As someone once said, "Let go and let God." Depend on Him to aid you in pursuing the destiny that He has for you. Taking matters into your own hands can result in your looking for answers or guidance in all the wrong places.

When I was in the eighth grade, the majorettes were the coolest, most beautiful, and most popular girls in school. After the day's classes were finished, these girls would meet out on the football field dressed in those cute little blue costumes and practice their twirling. The head majorette had a blue-and-gold sash across her shoulder, and all the majorettes had matching tassels on their white boots.

The boots—don't get me started—had metal cleats on the bottoms so that everyone knew when a majorette came into homeroom.

Great hair opens doors for you on the baton squad, and those girls seemed to have perfect hair. Some were blonde, others brunette. The head majorette, Heather-Megan Marie, had a rich chestnut-brown, waist-length mane. I had English class with Heather-Megan, and she always threw back that beautiful head of hair when she laughed. Whenever she came to class, she was surrounded by the other majorettes. They traveled in a pack, and all of them were gorgeous. They also had great names, like Jennifer, Nicole, Kara, Madison, and Kennedy. There was not an Ethel, Mabel, or Nora Irene among them. I wondered whether giving them really cool names made them really cool in life.

By the time I figured out that being a majorette was the ticket to being popular, it was already too late. My name was Cathy Lee Rothert, a decidedly normal name. Not hideous, but not exactly thrilling, like Kathleen or Catherine or Caitlin maybe, with an equally cool middle name such as Drew, Dylan, or some unisex name. I was Cathy, and my best friends were Sharon, Debbie, and Virginia. We were not majorettes, cheerleaders, or anything else that would have made any of our lives turn out differently, or so I thought.

Being sensitive to my situation, my precious mother found someone who taught baton twirling and enrolled me in the class. At a dollar a lesson, it made a huge dent in my baby-sitting funds. I showed up for my first lesson, and the class of eight was made up of first- and second-grade girls. All of them had great hair, and the most popular one's name was Allison. There we all stood in a line with our batons. Mine was new and shiny, a fact that I now really regret because all eight six-year-olds just stared at me.

The teacher, Mrs. Baxter, whose name sounded *so* familiar, introduced the student teacher to us. It was her daughter, Heather-Megan Marie Baxter. I wanted to die. Now everyone in the school would know that I was taking baton lessons with the pee-wee class.

What was worse was that the majorettes would know that I was taking lessons. I was mortified. I am not sure if I was being laughed at when I walked into English class the next morning or not, but I felt the stares and heard the giggles. Sporting a purple bruise on my forehead from hitting myself in the head with my shining baton, I had spent the morning trying to cover it up. But alas, I do not have majorette hair. I have fine, straight hair that lies a little flat ten minutes after I take the curlers out.

Dear reader, my career as a majorette was short-lived. After exactly one lesson, the baton went into the back of my closet until my eight-year-old brother found it. He took off the rubber end caps, tied a pillowcase to it, and used it to carry rocks and bugs and anything else he could think of. It was just as well.

Next I tried dancing, but I did not display the ability to coordinate my arms with my feet. If desire and heart counted, I would have been the prima ballerina with the American Ballet Company in New York. My heart was right, but my body was spastic. I was not attractive to watch. I did no better in cheerleading, color guard, rifle drill team, or girls' volleyball.

One day, my ever-faithful mother gently suggested I try out for the school chorus. There I found my calling. It was a matter of finding the gift that God had given me and then developing that talent. I hit pay dirt when I joined the drama club. Within two years I was president and had the female lead in all the school musicals. During tryouts I would watch with satisfaction as pep club members or junior varsity cheerleaders sang off-key. I still wished I was one of them, but I realize now that I was trying to be someone I was not, just to please others. It is frustrating to try and try, only to be told you are not wanted or needed.

We respond to failure, rejection, and inadequacy in many ways, but you can take this to the bank: emotionally healthy and well-grounded people recognize that maybe twirling a baton or having the solo or becoming a hockey star is not their role to play. Not because they are horrible people and there is a government plot to destroy them, but because they are not coordinated or lack the necessary skills. They learn to see that they have a different role in the play—one that they can handle with skill and excellence.

> Ask yourself whether your dreams were conceived by you alone or instilled in you by the Holy Spirit.

I learned a valuable lesson concerning the pursuit of dreams. Usually grasping your dream and living it are much easier if your dream is something you are fairly good at doing. In my case, it was acting and singing. It is also essential to ask yourself whether your dreams were conceived by you alone or instilled in you by the Holy Spirit. You may have a burning passion to tell people about Jesus, but not everyone is called to spend her life preaching in China.

A Fairy-Tale Destiny

A single woman named Ginny used to go to the same prayer meeting that I attended. Ginny had the most generous heart. She would have done anything for anyone and often did. She wanted more than anything to have a huge home and have a family with about five kids. But at fifty-eight years of age, and after experiencing two divorces and undergoing a hysterectomy, she was unable to have children.

Then one day at a large gathering of women, Ginny announced that God told her she was going to get pregnant and have twins. She already had picked out their names. She also said that she was believing God for a two-million-dollar home that she had seen for sale.

No one at that conference said a word until . . .

All of a sudden, a lady who clearly was troubled jumped up and began to prophesy: "I hear the Lord saying, 'Yes, daughter, I will give you that house. It won't even cost you any money. The owners will just give the keys to you. You will get pregnant twice with twins, and you will travel all over the world with them. It will be a sign and wonder that, without even a husband, you will give birth to these babies.'"

Oh, brother! Talk about putting a damper on a meeting!

What was so sad was that several of the girls who were new Christians believed her, and when we pointed out the fact that there was only one Immaculate Conception, we were accused of trying to discourage Ginny and steal her faith for her miracle.

That was seventeen years ago, and none of those things ever happened. Ginny lives alone, without children, in a used mobile home that she rents for $345 a month. She has almost been evicted twice. She gets someone to pay her rent and refuses to work because "God told her not to." She needs to be free to take care of the mansion and the twins.

Now, that is a very extreme example of someone who has a fairy-tale destiny that will never come to pass. But I know others who hold on to dreams that are equally silly, yet refuse to take counsel or entertain the thought that their destinies might be different from what they originally thought.

Your Destiny

My dreams have changed with the years. I no longer daydream about being called Heather and twirling for the Macy's Thanksgiving Day Parade. I have also allowed the Lord to adjust my dream of being married to an Irish tenor and bearing six sons. It is certainly not a lack of faith that has been responsible for the change. In fact, my faith has continued to keep dreams alive in my heart. This life I now live is a great deal more exciting than anything that I could possibly have dreamed up. Believe me, the reality is much more thrilling than the imagination.

So be content with your great destiny, and keep praying for those things unfulfilled. If you trust in God, you will find that your destiny will fall into place, and you won't waste countless years trying to be someone you are not.

Meanwhile, meet me behind the high school. And don't forget to bring your boots and baton. When you get there, just ask for Heather.

Chapter Sixteen

Focus on the Journey, Not the Destination!

O ur family's collective goal that summer was to spit in the Grand Canyon. To achieve that objective, our father made us get up at "dark-thirty." Our clothes were already laid out the night before, shoes and socks at the foot of the bed, so we would not lose thirty seconds of driving time if we waited until the morning to pick them out. The car had been packed the night before. There were sandwiches made and put into a cooler that sat on the floorboard under my feet so precious time wasn't wasted getting off the high-way for food.

Five of us piled into the green Dodge (my father always bought Dodge automobiles), and off we went. Racing against the sunset and heading west, Dad always loved it when we made "good time"—no matter where we were driving in the car. God forbid if anyone had to go wee-wee. You were always asked to wait just a few more minutes. Couldn't you hold it until the exit? No, we couldn't. As much as it pained him, he finally pulled off the road, opened both doors on the right side of the car to shield us from oncoming traffic, and tapped his ring on the steering wheel while we squatted on the side of the road. I don't know about you, but it's difficult to "go" when cars are whizzing by at seventy-five miles per hour with all of the occupants knowing what you're doing.

Inevitably by two o'clock in the afternoon, the whining started: "I'm hungry. I'm tired. I've got to go again. Can we please stop at a motel with a pool? Please, please, Mom tell Dad." We appealed to our mother as if our parents were not sitting six inches away from each other. She would wait about fifteen minutes so it didn't seem so obvious that she felt the same way we did and then begin pointing out motel billboards along the highway.

"That's a good one, Dad. It has a pool. Turn here, Dad . . . Dad . . . *Dad!* You missed it. Here, Dad, this one is better. It has a pool and a vibrating bed."

To the best of my recollection, it went on ad infinitum until Dad finally pulled over and stopped.

All I really wanted to do was to get to the motel, put on my new vacation bathing suit, rush out to the pool, and try to grab the eye of a gorgeous boy at each stop. My parents always vacationed with their best friends every summer, and their daughter was my best friend. We had our own collective goal, and it was to get a cute guy to notice us. When you are thirteen and fourteen years old, everything is about you.

The year we went to the Grand Canyon turned out to be the last family vacation we would ever take together. I didn't know it then.

I would have been nicer to my little brother instead of threatening to throw him over the east wall because he . . . Well, I don't really remember why, except he got on my nerves. Sorry, Harold.

To get to the Grand Canyon, we drove four days only to arrive right before they closed the park. Can you believe it? We all jumped out, ran to the rim, spit, then jumped back into the car and raced three and a half days to get back home. Dad made really great time in the Dodge.

The Adventure Is in the Journey

All pilgrims need to understand one critical factor when they are stretching to reach their dream. They need to know that after they determine what their destiny is, what God is calling them and directing them to achieve, their objective must not be the destination; rather, they must learn to focus on and enjoy the journey.

One of the more cruel attacks of the enemy in our lives occurs when he deceives us into living only for the achieving of the goal rather than learning to live successfully "in the moment." When we focus on the goal, so often it becomes a source of frustration because it is always "out there." The carrot is just too far away to be grasped, and the result is often weariness and misery because of our failure to grasp the prize. Among the thousands of men and women I meet each year, I see this all the time, and frankly I have been guilty of the same thing.

We become so excited at the possibility of God's changing our situation. We can see by the eye of faith the great plan that awaits us. The Lord shows us these things by revealing His word to us in many different ways. But if the enemy can get us to give up or tempt us with discouragement because of the "devilish delay," then he wins.

Often if that type of attack does not work, Satan tries another tactic. He attempts to sway our minds into comparing the present reality with the future promise. I guarantee you that your present will always look miserable when you look at the end promise. And that can be especially trying when you are trusting God in the arena of physical reality is pain, and future promise seems so unattainable because there is no release from the pain cycle. Of course, this can be fertile ground for discouragement, and if the seeds are allowed to root in you, then you can easily become subject to depression and unbelief.

> If you live only for the fulfillment, you will miss one of the greatest of life's joys—the joy of the journey.

What a devastating turnaround! Instead of the promise of your future being exciting, it now serves up depression for dessert. So what was your dream is now an "impossible dream." The psalmist talked about "songs in the night," but they were not the sounds of a comforting melody from God. One of the proverbs declared, "Hope deferred makes the heart sick" (Prov. 13:12).

The answer for you, dear sister, is to realize that the joy is in the journey as well as in the fulfillment of the dream. On the journey, you learn to trust and conquer through the presence and power of God at work in you. Remember, if you live only for the fulfillment, you will miss one of the greatest of life's joys—the joy of the journey.

On the journey you learn to trust in Jesus. We all have room for improvement in the trusting department. The journey is where you fall deeper in love with Jesus. You cannot avoid the journey; it is necessary to get to the destination, but it is not to be merely endured or dreaded. God is with you. He is your Fortress and High Tower.

I can look back on the times in my life when, somehow by God's grace, I have grown and increased in wisdom. In retrospect, often those were times when I found myself right in the middle of a wilderness. In the process of God's getting you to the land of promise, you must make the journey through the wilderness. As much as I do not relish desert experiences, I do recognize that the hand of God was increased on my life and it was directly related to pressing through the dry places. Isn't that exciting? I know, not really, huh?

By the way, talking about desert experiences, my dad was famous for his shortcuts. Most of the time he thought maps were for sissies and foreigners. On the way back from the Grand Canyon, on a "shortcut" we passed through New Mexico. Don't ask me how we got there, please! We ended up in a little diner that featured a huge buffalo head on the wall. The look in his eyes (I think it was a he) was one of total surprise and shock. We all took turns guessing what the buffalo's last words were. My older brother's guess was the best: "Can you believe it? I thought they bought me to be the family pet."

I am sure, dear reader, that you have some wonderful memories of family trips, exciting vacations, and the making of new friends on these journeys. Please try to remember that in your passionate desire to capture your dream—the special destiny that God has embedded in your heart—there will be many obstacles and frustrations that will block your path. But it is a journey, one that lasts a lifetime.

Give this some thought, too: most of the time you will not travel alone. Other pilgrims will be there to give you encouragement and the occasional boost that we all need. The bottom line, however, is this fact: "I am with you always, even unto the ends of the earth." That's the promise of God for all of us.

Whatever Is in You Will Come A-Squishing Out When You Get Stepped On

We all realize that God knows everything about us. He is able to keep track of the number of hairs that fall out of our heads and go down the shower drain. Can't you just see the angel who has been assigned to you with a clipboard in his hands watching over you and mumbling to himself, "Twenty-two thousand nine hundred and sixty-two . . . no, twenty-two thousand nine hundred and sixty-one"?

I wonder, though, if the angels rotate because that must be an awful job, being the hair angel. I would want to be the vacation angel, the one who is in charge of protecting you from getting sunburn in Tahiti.

So if God allows and even directs your path through the wilderness, what would be His intention in taking you through this part of the journey? He wants *you* to see what is inside so that you will see for yourself how fully dedicated you are to follow Him.

Just as Moses was taken from the cushy life of the palace as an adopted son of Pharaoh and got dumped in the wilderness of Midian, so we, too, can experience something similar via the good hand of our Father. Midian was basically the backside of the desert, and Moses went from being served in the royal palace to being a shepherd toiling in the sun every day. When Moses left the palace, he did so in great disgrace. He had killed a man and had to get out of town before anyone found out. But God already knew this man Moses. He had called him as a child. God also knew Moses' character flaws. I think the man's huge temper eventually might have destroyed him. So, God took him to the wilderness and started to fashion him through the difficulties of his journey.

> **He wants you to see what is inside so that you will see for yourself how fully dedicated you are to follow Him.**

Not only did Moses' anger erupt, taking the life of an Egyptian, but he was always striking something. The rock, the tablets containing the Ten Commandments, and the golden calf all felt the brunt of his rage. God had the perfect solution. He dumped Moses in the middle of nowhere in a lousy job. I am quite sure that during those forty years Moses must have felt abandoned and that his dream to somehow redeem God's people Israel would probably never come to pass.

That is the temptation for us as we make our journey—to quit when the victory is obscure or the finish line is not evident, even though it may be just around the corner. The man who emerged from the wilderness of Midian was not the same man who went into the wilderness. God had "stepped on him" so that Moses could get a glimpse from God's perspective of the changes needed in his character.

King David, the sweet psalmist, was another example of God's using the journey to prepare him for the throne. Both Moses and David, however, had serious character flaws that needed correction. God got involved and helped them in the difficult process.

Faith Laughs

Another lesson while you travel is learning how to enjoy the journey. Life can be full of tremendous heartache at times. If you don't have to cry, then don't. Laughter is better than two Tylenol tablets. You are not ignoring the situation, but you are looking at the end victory "by faith," and faith laughs. Isn't that what Abraham's wife, Sarah, did? She was promised a son when she didn't even have a cycle anymore, and the idea seemed ludicrous. She laughed, got pregnant, and gave birth to her son. For some reason I have a hard time imagining a ninety-year-old woman in a pair of maternity jeans and a red top that says BABY with an arrow pointing down to her belly. On the journey, pilgrim, laughter can carry you over many a mile of difficulties and concerns. The Word is trustworthy. I believe it happened.

This brings us to another wilderness lesson: Sarah bought herself a load of sorrow and grief when she failed to learn the lessons of faith in her journey. Because she did not believe the specific promise the Lord gave to her husband—that she would get pregnant in old age and have a special son—she concocted an elaborate plan to have her maid become a surrogate mother for her and Abraham. She did not, on that occasion, trust God. Remember this little adage: if God fixes a fix to fix you, and you just fix the fix that God fixed to fix you, that's okay, because He'll just fix another fix and then He will fix you. I know, a bit of a tongue twister, but say it five times real fast, and it will start to make sense to you.

In other words the heavenly Father who loves you so desperately knows that if He allows you to remain in the condition that you are in right now, you may never see the great prophetic plan come to pass. Stop resisting, and begin cooperating with God's plan for your life. You have it in your power to choose to cooperate with God and seize these destiny moments to get on the road to completing the dreams He has placed in your heart.

Epilogue

How do I want to leave you at the conclusion of this book? I have been diligently seeking the face of God for a way to encourage you to continue pressing on. Your destiny in God is worth anything and everything you must suffer to obtain it. I hope you strongly believe this now that you have just about completed reading this book. Here is a little word to the wise.

When you run the race with patience to obtain the prize, there are others who are affected by your efforts. Take, for example, this book. I prayed and cried out to the Lord before I ever agreed to undertake writing it. Why? Because I have written five previous books, and I understand the sacrifice it requires to birth a book of substance. I understand the sacrifice of family time, the hours spent behind closed doors telling my children, "Sorry, sweetheart, not now. Mommy's writing," and hearing their little sighs.

But when I asked the Lord if this book was part of the destiny He had for me, He simply spoke into my spirit and said, *Write the book.*

I hope that by my obedience to His words, you are also encouraged to pay the price and continue in the pursuit of His calling. And what a calling you have. Young or old, rich or poor, simple or sophisticated, it matters not when you respond to God's call with your "Here I am, Father, send me."

Bringing forth your destiny is much like going through childbirth. In a certain sense, you are pregnant with the seed of the Word of God that has been planted and cultivated in your life. Just as in the physical realm the seed must be fertilized with the sperm of the father, the Word of God in you must also be fertilized in order to bring forth life. Remember this Word in you is "the power of God unto salvation," it is "the lamp for your feet and the light for your path," and it is the hidden seed in your heart that will keep you from sin and a whole lot more. This is the potential life-giving power within you, the divine seed of God.

I saw a documentary on the Learning Channel in which two doctors were discussing the cycle of a healthy woman of childbearing age. One doctor pointed out that in a woman's twenty-eight-day cycle there is a window of two days when she is at optimum fertility. The other doctor added that, out of those two days of optimum fertility, there are really only two hours when conception is most likely to occur. The body fluid in a woman actually repels the sperm at all other times during the month. But in those two target hours, her body fluid changes, and the fluid actually assists in fertilization. The woman's egg puts on a little Victoria's Secret negligee with matching red high heels and begins the dance of the seven veils. One little sperm is handing out cigars before he knows what hit him.

You, too, have a window of opportunity in which the Spirit of God desires to come and fertilize the seed of God's Word within you. As He does this, you will be empowered to give life to others in the name of Jesus. Hidden with Christ in God, you will have the opportunity to dream dreams, see visions, and bear much fruit. That is your destiny, dear friend. But before this new life, there must come the birth and with it, the labor and the pains of delivery.

I Didn't Know It Would Hurt This Bad

When I was pregnant with my oldest child, I informed everyone that I would be having natural childbirth. No drugs would pass through *me* into my unborn baby. My husband and I took lessons at the local hospital. During each class, I practiced my breathing techniques, knowing that in a couple of hours I would be sitting at Denny's eating a monstrous British burger with extra cheese and heavy onions.

But practicing for labor and delivery is a lot different from experiencing the real thing. I don't know what could have been said to me that would have prepared me for the worst pain known to humanity. Maybe if they had pulled out my fingernails or drilled my teeth without Novocain . . .

Unless a mother has a cesarean, there is only one way to get the baby out. It is like pushing a refrigerator out of your ear. A woman must transition from zero to ten centimeters to deliver the baby. By seven centimeters I was standing on the bed, begging for any drug available. I wanted morphine, heroin, *and* cocaine. I wanted the stuff they save for the dying. And I wanted it *now!*

All those breathing lessons, out the window. I was giving birth, it hurt, and I was pretty mad. I decided not to have children after all. I would be a cat lady instead. But the hospital does not look kindly on a whale-sized woman leaving the hospital with all the medical equipment still attached.

Many women who do not want the commitment have aborted their unborn babies. Too many Christians abort their great destinies because they never counted on the intensity of the pain. They quit and start over again and again, becoming more discouraged each time because they have nothing to show for their hurt.

That is why the Word is filled with admonishments to stand, not to faint. Don't give up; don't get weary in well doing. Not me and not you, my friend.

Getting pregnant is the easy part. Carrying it to term, maintaining a forgiving and sweet spirit during delivery, and then raising that promise to maturity, well, that requires your entire life. What else have you got to do?

You can do it. You *will* do it. So take my hand, and when the pain gets hard, squeeze. You will be so happy when it's all over and you are holding this beautiful baby in your arms.

> Hope deferred makes the heart sick,
> But when the desire comes, it is a tree of life. (Prov. 13:12)

Just think, even with fat thighs, all new mothers look beautiful!

Acknowledgments

This is the most fun part of the book for me, but also the most neglected. Many people skip over this part unless they think they might be mentioned. Well, what if you are mentioned and you don't read it and I meet you somewhere this year and ask you what you thought about the stuff I wrote about you in the acknowledgments? Wow, that could be a potential disaster. So, you will just have to read on.

My wonderful children try so hard to understand why Mommy is sitting on the floor with their school writing paper and those big, fat, chubby purple crayons, trying to write a book. (Because said children lost Mommy's good writing notebook after they filled it with pictures of spaceships, monsters, cats, and the alphabet in cursive.)

You have never really had a challenge unless you have tried to meet a deadline with a three-year-old on your lap. Every second word you write looks like *Jesus wermsxwo then uywqqqq*. But those children are the joys of my life.

Jerusha Rose, my twenty-four-year-old whose encouragement is priceless, and eight-year-old Hannah Ruth, who is bright, creative, funny, and smart beyond her natural years.

Gabriel Levi, you are my comforter. When everyone has left, you always come back to tell me I look like I need some extra hugs. Remember how I told you that you couldn't marry until you are thirty-five? I was just kidding. You can leave when you're thirty-three.

Samuel Josiah, my third eight-year-old, my little prince, my bodyguard. Everyone thinks you are such a toughie, but Mommy knows what incredible gentleness and tenderness you possess that are so much more than the tough part.

Abagael Elisha, my princess, my ballerina who moves with such grace. I cannot imagine living my life without you in it. At six, you stand head and shoulders above everyone else, and I see that quality in the spirit as well.

My Lydia Danielle, a five-year-old who thinks she is fifteen. Every family has one. Lydia, you have the most amazing heart. You have a capacity to love and to nurture. You can't stand it if any one of your baby dolls is sick. I understand when you tell me that when you grow up, you are going to be a "baby rocker."

Hadassah Rose, our baby. Well, you are actually three, but Daddy's eyes light up when you come into the room. We will never forget when you stood on a dining room chair to sing a song of worship over dinner one night and belted out "Grandma got run over by a reindeer, walking home from our house Christmas Eve." Life with you will never be boring.

My gorgeous husband, Randi, who has stuck by me every step of the way. His insight and wisdom, even when I really didn't care for the answer, were usually right. Thank you for being secure enough in your own call to release me to fulfill mine.

Erin Yancey who is more than my secretary. She is a Ruth to my Naomi, but even more of a Jonathan to my David, Huck Finn to my Tom Sawyer, Ren to my Stimpy, Ethel to my Lucy, Patrick to my Sponge Bob Square Pants, Robin to my Batman, that other girl to Xena Warrior Princess . . . somebody stop me!

Paulette Donaldson, Johanna Oramas, Jackie Austin, and all those who realize that this is more than a job, it is a ministry. Thank you for the part you do in order for me to do mine. I love you very much.

Aaron Rothert, my gorgeous nephew.

Victor Oliver for seeing in me something great and nurturing it.

My mother, Rose Rothert, for your labor in deciphering my chicken scratch, for not yelling at me too much when I wait until the last minute and pile a ton of work on you. For displaying courage and kindness after the loss of your beloved husband. You have given a living example for your children and grandchildren to follow. What a legacy!

Dr. Carmen Vivero, who has the most incredible love and compassion for God's servants. Thanks for taking care of me.

Lisa, Rachel, and Yolanda Smith—you always know just the right thing to do and I will be in your debt for your constant selflessness.

All those who pray for me, my grandmother Ruth, Ann Taylor, Michele Lomax, and Thelma Ducharme.

I saved the best for last. Jesus, You are my reason for being. You have seen me through an incredible year, and I am grateful that You love me. You repay with kindness when I'm impatient; You look through eyes of love in all Your judgments. May this book and my life be a sure sign to the world that there is hope for them.

About the Author

Cathy Lechner is the daughter of an Assemblies of God minister. Being raised in the church, she was well prepared for life as a pastor's wife. She is the wife of Randi and, along with their seven children, Jerusha Rose, Hannah Ruth, Gabriel Levi, Samuel Josiah, Abagael Elisha, Lydia Danielle, and Hadassah Rose, lives in Jacksonville, Florida.

Cathy teaches the Word of God with great joy and power. Her humor is disarming, allowing listeners to both laugh and cry as they are challenged in their walk with the Lord. She moves in the Word of knowledge and in a strong prophetic anointing.

She has spoken at numerous women's conferences and churches across the country. The Lord has graciously used her to touch and heal hundreds of lives in Far Eastern countries, Central America, Puerto Rico, Russia, England, and Australia.

Cathy is also the author of *I'm Trying to Sit at His Feet, but Who's Going to Cook Dinner?*; *Can't We Kill 'Em and Tell God They Died?*; *I Hope God's Promises Come to Pass Before My Body Parts Go South*; *You've Got to Be Kidding, I Thought This WAS the Great Tribulation!*; and *I'm Tired of Crying, It's Time to Laugh Again!*

Read these books by other women with a heart for Christ...

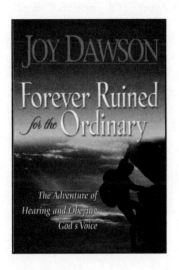

Forever Ruined for the Ordinary

Beloved speaker Joy Dawson describes what happened when she decided to follow God with an obedient heart: "I was tuned in and turned on to God, the Creator and Sustainer of the universe. I took off on an adventure of a lifetime . . . hearing and obeying God's voice. I was forever ruined for the ordinary." Emphasizing God's commitment to be personally involved in our lives, Joy shares the lessons of a lifetime of faithful obedience to God.
ISBN: 0-7852-6682-8

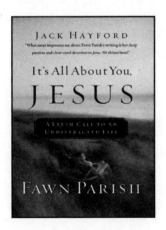

It's All About You, Jesus

In modern Christendom, religious catchphrases and spiritual slogans abound, but too often these buzzwords are a smoke screen for lives without substance. At best, they are the peripherals that threaten to overshadow the one thing we truly need . . . more intimacy with Jesus. In *It's All About You, Jesus,* Fawn Parish offers fresh insight on the distorted emphasis on worship in our churches and how we can change it.
ISBN: 0-7852-6612-7

Let Prayer Change Your Life Workbook

If you struggle between desiring a meaningful prayer life and actually having one, this workbook is for you. Becky Tirabassi's unique system of prayer journaling has enriched the prayer lives of thousands. This repackaged and updated companion workbook to the bestselling *Let Prayer Change Your Life* is an easy-to-use and fulfilling approach to developing a prayer life that works. ISBN: 0-7852-6658-5

The View From Goose Ridge

What do barn cats, manure in a field, a pygmy goat, a lonely horse, a muddy pond, and pruning have in common? They offer lessons of grace from the life of Cheryl Bostrom, columnist for the Women of Faith Web site (which gets more than 1 million page views a month). *The View from Goose Ridge* offers a refreshing look at the changing seasons in a woman's life—and a wise perspective on living a life of faith with grace and gentleness. ISBN: 0-7852-6655-0